Crusade for Liberation

OTHER BOOKS BY THE AUTHOR

Freedom and Unity/Uhuru na Umoja
(A selection from writings and speeches 1952-1965)

Freedom and Socialism/Uhuru na Ujamaa
(A selection from writings and speeches 1965-1967)

Nyerere on Socialism
(The collected Introductions to the above two works)

Ujamaa – Essays on Socialism
(A selection from *Freedom and Socialism/Uhuru na Ujamaa*)

Ujamaa
(The Swahili version of *Ujamaa – Essays on Socialism*)

Freedom and Development/Uhuru na Maendeleo
(A selection from writings and speeches 1968-1973)

Man and Development
(A selection from *Freedom and Development/Uhuru na Maendeleo*)

Swahili Translations

Juliasi Kaizari
(Shakespeare's *Julius Caesar*)

Mabepari wa Venisi
(Shakespeare's *The Merchant of Venice*)

JULIUS K. NYERERE

Crusade for Liberation

Introductory material by
the Press Office, State House,
Dar es Salaam

Dar es Salaam
OXFORD UNIVERSITY PRESS
Nairobi Oxford New York

Oxford University Press

OXFORD LONDON GLASGOW
NEW YORK TORONTO MELBOURNE WELLINGTON
IBADAN NAIROBI DAR ES SALAAM CAPE TOWN
KUALA LUMPUR SINGAPORE JAKARTA HONG KONG TOKYO
DELHI BOMBAY CALCUTTA MADRAS KARACHI

Oxford University Press, P.O. Box 5299, Dar es Salaam, Tanzania

Made and printed in Tanzania

ISBN 0 19 572462 3

To the struggling peoples of
southern Africa

ONE

IT IS twenty past noon, on 2 November 1976. Here at Lindi, in southern Tanzania, the President of the United Republic of Tanzania, Mwalimu Julius Nyerere, has just emerged from chairing a meeting of his Tanganyika African National Union Executive Committee.

Routine business, you might think, for a man who has been President of TANU since he founded it a little over twenty-two years ago. But this has been no ordinary National Executive Committee meeting. It has just gone through and approved the text of a constitution for a new Party, merging mainland Tanzania's TANU and Zanzibar's Afro-Shiraz Party into a single powerful political party.

To the Union of Tanganyika and Zanzibar, which came into being on 26 April 1964, the decision to merge the two Parties was a step of immense significance, in the consolidation of the Union. To the struggle for the liberation of southern Africa, it is a major filip. To balkanized Africa, this is yet another* effective pointer to the fact that African unity is not out of reach of a determined people.

It is fittingly a day of great rejoicing for the members of TANU. For after this only three other steps lie ahead before the merger can be effected—similar approval of the constitution by the A.S.P.'s National Executive Committee, its approval by the National Executive Committees of both parties and ratification by a joint TANU and A.S.P. Conference.

As founder of TANU, continuously elected to its presidency and now standing in the threshold of becoming a founding member of Tanzania's new single political party, Julius Nyerere is undoubtedly the happiest person in Lindi this afternoon.

Yet as other members of the National Executive go off jubilating over their approval of the Constitution, Nyerere quickly drives back to his lodge, in order to up-date

---

* Tanganyika and Zanzibar are the only two African countries so far to have come together to form a union.

himself on developments taking place that day in a far off nation, and over which he has neither say nor control, but which are nevertheless of great interest to Tanzania and Africa. The people of the United States of America are electing their President. Theoretically, American presidential elections should bear the same significance to Tanzanians and Africa as any other similar elections elsewhere in the world. But given its powerful position in the world today and the enormous influence the United States exercises over the daily lives of millions of people outside the U.S., American presidential elections are that different!

Today's elections bear even greater significance, to Tanzania and Africa, as far as concerns the liberation struggle in southern Africa, because of the declared policies of the two candidates. Incumbent President Gerry Ford is seeking his first* mandate from the American electorate to lead that country for a full, four-year term.

His policies towards southern Africa, as articulated by his Secretary of State, Henry Kissinger, have been seeing the liberation struggle in southern Africa basically as aimed at handing the continent over to the Soviet Union. America's belated interest in a solution to the racial and colonial problems in southern Africa as demonstrated by Kissinger's shuttles of April through September 1976 was basically to police, contain and finally counteract this 'Soviet threat'.

James Earl Carter, the Democratic presidential candidate on the other hand, has been described on many occasions as an 'unknown quantity'. But during the campaign, Carter makes pronouncements about the liberation struggle in southern Africa, which indicate that he does not regard the struggle as one whose objective is to hand over Africa to the Soviet Union, just because Africa is a recipient of Soviet arms.

So although Julius Nyerere has neither say nor influence on how the American people are going to vote today, he is nonetheless intensely interested in the outcome of the election. For this will determine whether it is going to be another four years with an America which sees the struggle

* Gerry Ford had not been elected to the Presidency. He was nominated by outgoing President Richard Nixon and approved by Congress.

as being about the removal of western colonialism and west-supported racial systems and a hand-over to the Soviet Union, or whether there will be an understanding American administration.

To the extent that these are the choices, the election has generated an understandable amount of anxiety in Julius Nyerere's mind. And this is further compounded by the fact that pre-election polls in the United States itself have shown Carter's earlier comfortable lead steadily melt away as the polling day approaches. Reputable radio stations are this afternoon reporting a neck-and-neck election, to be determined only by such unpredictables as the weather on polling day.

So for the whole of this afternoon in Lindi, Nyerere and his aides are patiently following the election day happenings through the radio. There is a long moment of anxiety when one of the radio stations reports that President Ford has finally just managed to wipe out Jimmy Carter's marginal lead and is in fact leading him by one per cent. The tension persists until later on when the station drops this as its lead story and completely omits any further mention of this item.

But Lindi and Washington are separated by a time difference of eight hours. And at the time the President and his aides retire, close to midnight (Tanzanian time), it is only four o'clock in the afternoon in eastern United States and as early as just about noon in the U.S. west coast!

All that the President is able to get before retiring is that there has been a big turn-out that election morning. And a big turn-out, political analysts have said, will tend to favour Jimmy Carter than it will Ford. Neither here nor there really!

So there is Nyerere, Chairman of that grouping of Front Line States which, on behalf of the Organization of African Unity, has been charged with the close supervision and co-ordination of the liberation struggle in southern Africa, going to spend the night in this uncertain state of affairs.

Come the morning of 3 November. Aides are up extraordinarily early today to catch up with overnight developments. Lindi, unlike Dar es Salaam, the capital, lacks good means of mass communication. The only access to the outside world available in Lindi this morning is the radio, never mind the reception.

By breakfast it is reported that the early results show a substantial lead by Carter. What hopes this generates are sobbered up by oft-repeated views of observers of the American electoral processes that leads which build up from the early Eastern results are often inconclusive. They can be and often are erased when results come in from the Midwest and Western states.

Carter continues to be ahead of Ford in bulletin after bulletin this morning. But balanced against previous experiences, the situation remains fluid well into the latter part of the morning when Nyerere flies out to Dar es Salaam on his way to Zanzibar for the joint TANU/A.S.P. N.E.C. meeting to study the new Constitution, which TANU's N.E.C. has just approved.

The one-hour plane journey effectively cuts off the President and his aides from the running reports on the election news being carried by radio stations around the world. On arrival at his Msasani home, tension gives way to hope when one of the three major American television networks reports computer projections showing Jimmy Carter as winning the election. Hope gives way to excitement when a second network comes up with similar computer results. Then bang on comes the third !

It is an ecstatic moment when an official announcement is put out on the Voice of America naming James Earl Carter as the thirty-ninth President of the United States of America. President Nyerere, who, in the continuing tension, had sought quiet and solitude in the upstairs quarters of his home, descends and joins his aides, in a toast for a better U.S. understanding of if nothing else, the liberation struggle in southern Africa ! 'I think this is good news for Africa,' he remarks.

.This rejoicing was surely not in vain. For shortly after his inauguration on 20 January 1977, Jimmy Carter made President Nyerere his first choice of an African leader to be invited over to Washington for talks on southern Africa.

Nyerere accepts the invitation. He goes straight into preparations for yet another crusade for the liberation of southern Africa. He calls a summit of the Front Line Presidents to map out strategy on his Washington talks.

That done he sets off for the week-long crusade covering a total of 32 000 miles in 55 hours of flying.

Nyerere arrives in Washington in the afternoon of 3 August. At Andrew's Air Force Base, he is received by an enthusiastic line-up of African diplomats and students, who have correctly perceived his visit as a crusade for American support for the liberation struggle in the racist-dominated and colonized southern Africa.

Washington protocol requires that visiting Heads of State are received by their host on the grounds of the White House, not at the airport. So Mwalimu is escorted to the Government Guest Quarters, Blair House, where he is to stay for the three nights he spends in Washington.

At the White House in the morning of 4 August, President Nyerere is met by President Jimmy Carter and his wife Rosalyn, and the Vice-President, Walter Mondale. A large crowd of enthusiastic citizens has negotiated its way into the White House lawns to see and hear Nyerere. Protocol arrangements succeed to do no more than separate this from the official line up which is in danger of being over-run by the lively crowd.

The usual twenty-one gun salute booms from across the impeccably-kept green lawns. The National Anthems are played. The guard of honour is on hand for President Nyerere to review. Then President Carter welcomes President Nyerere to America.

Fourteen years ago a young leader of our own nation, John Kennedy, welcomed a young leader of a new nation, Julius Nyerere, to our country.

There was a sharing of ideals and hopes and a mutual declaration of frustration about the hatred and racial discrimination and deprivation of the poor prevalent throughout the world.

It was an honour for our country to have this new leader come to see us when his own country was only two years old. He is a man who has come from a small village with a father who shaped his concepts about caring for those who need help and public service, a mother who kept the family close together in times of trial and tribulation when it was dangerous to express one's views about political change—a man who has deep religious convictions and who has been successful in his own country in translating those convictions into demonstrable concern about freedom, justice, equality, the alleviation of hunger, poverty and disease.

Now this same man, President Nyerere, from Tanzania, comes back to our nation, still a strong leader who in his country is known as teacher. He epitomizes what his country is, what it stands for. But now he is much more than a national leader—he is a wise man, experienced, a super politician who recognizes that the structure of government can be used for beneficial purposes. He is admired in every country by world leaders throughout this globe, a senior statesman whose integrity is unquestioned and which never has been questioned—a man who has foregone material wealth and ease in a sacrificial way for his own people.

In the troubled continent of Africa, he is recognized as pre-eminent in his commitment to the hopes and purposes of free people. He is a well-educated man, a scholar, a philosopher, a great writer, one who probes for new ideas and who expresses them succinctly and clearly to shape the minds of other people in a beneficent and constructive way.

Our own nation is deeply concerned about and with Africa. As a new President myself, I need his advice and his counsel and his friendship and his guidance as we try to act in a responsible and constructive fashion to bring about peace with justice in the thirty or more nations in Africa in the years ahead.

He can help me and others take the right stand as we bring about proper change towards majority rule in Rhodesia, or Zimbabwe, in Namibia and in the alleviation of racial discrimination throughout the continent of Africa and the rest of the world.

I value his friendship and look forward today and tomorrow in having a chance to learn from him.

It is with a great sense of appreciation of what he is and a clear recognition of the honour bestowed upon our country by the visit of President Nyerere that I would like to say on behalf of the American people, Mr. President, welcome, or in your language, 'karibu'.

Nyerere moves over to the microphones. In a low, remarkably carrying and purposeful voice he replies to Carter.

Mr. President, you have been very generous in your remarks about myself and my country, and I do thank you with great sincerity for the warmth of your welcome to me and my colleagues. I can assure you that I have very great pleasure in coming to the United States at your invitation.

We in Tanzania—and in Africa generally—follow American politics with close attention. There is the intrinsic interest in the affairs of the most powerful nation the world has ever known; more to the point—your politics affect us! Indeed, we in Tanzania sometimes think that the world should somehow join in the process of electing the American President! For although we realize that the American people do not elect an Absolute Monarch, the world power structure is such that other peoples, and other nations, have a vital interest in the person whom the American people choose as their executive Head of State. We appreciate your recognition of this fact in the 'Message to Audiences Abroad' which you issued on your inauguration. Let me, therefore, once again offer you, Mr. President, our congratulations on the honour and the heavy responsibilty which the American people have given you. I am very happy to be in the White House today as your guest, just as I was the guest of your distinguished predecessor, and my friend, the late President Kennedy in 1963.

Mr. President, I am glad for this opportunity to discuss with you the matters of common interest between our two sovereign states, and particularly the problems of southern Africa. For we in Tanzania have greatly welcomed your administration's new approach to matters related to the liberation of my continent from colonialism and racialism.

I am therefore looking forward to my discussions with you and your colleagues, and with members of Congress. I am also very happy to have been invited to spend a few extra days in this country, and to have been given the opportunity to visit different parts of the country. I do not expect to become an expert on America from my brief visits to different states of the U.S.A., but I am sure that I shall learn a great deal of interest to me and my countrymen.

Thank you.

TWO

The formal welcome ceremonies are over. Nyerere and Carter head straight for talks. They agree to dwell exclusively on Zimbabwe on the first day reserving Namibia for the second. At the talks, Nyerere argues the case for majority rule in Zimbabwe. He specifically seeks to get American support for the removal of the illegal regime in Rhodesia, the dismantling of its army and its replacement by an army based on the liberation forces. He calls for elections based on one-man-one-vote as has all along been demanded by the Organization of African Unity and the international community. He seeks American support for Zimbabwe's independence in 1978. Nyerere finds a strikingly concordant note in these talks. Carter accepts all those points that Nyerere raises.

The talks are followed by a luncheon at the State Department hosted by Vice-President Mondale. Here the opportunity is taken to get to know the top administration officials and to further clarify issues.

True to form Nyerere loses no opportunity to mobilize support for the liberation struggle while in the United States. Soon after the lunch, he is receiving a stream of influential leaders of the American society: senators, civic leaders and congressmen. The message is consistent and unmistakable. 'Our cause is just; lend us your support. At the very least, do nothing to encourage the enemy.'

Carter that evening hosts a working dinner for Nyerere. Nyerere had earlier specifically sent word that he did not want the pomp and the glamour of a state banquet. That would detract from the seriousness of the business for which he was in the U.S.

Carter makes an unwritten speech in toasting Nyerere. He says:

Infrequently on the world scene, there arises a young leader at the beginning of the history of a nation who in a strange but all pervasive way represents what his people are and what his country hopes to be, and our guest here tonight is that kind of leader.

Fourteen years ago, he came here when his nation was two years old. He had been searching for a role of leadership in a sacrificial way. He came from a small town and came to visit our young President, John Kennedy, and they exchanged ideas about the future, and he honoured our country then by coming.

Now, our guest, President Nyerere of Tanzania, has come here as a distinguished senior citizen, still young in body and in spirit but experienced and respected and a man who, when he speaks, has others listen—a man of modesty and great achievement who in my opinion holds the key to the furthering of peace and equality of treatment and opportunity and freedom in Africa as dearly and closely as any person alive.

I am very honoured that he would come and meet with me today and tomorrow and visit us in the White House tonight.

I have been talking to him about groundnuts and life in the rural area and his struggle for a good education and what his religious life means to him and the impact of his father on his social consciousness, and I have learned a lot about him in the process.

We have a need for advice and counsel and co-operation and mutual support because the tremendous power of our country can be felt in the region of the world which is of great interest to President Nyerere.

The southern part of Africa, as you well know, is one that is troubled—where people are struggling to escape from the historical impact of colonialism and trying to do it peacefully.

We, like Tanzania, were formerly subjects of the British Crown, and we had a military victory to achieve independence—Tanzania had a victory in a peaceful fashion. We now see other nations struggling for their own independence where their own people might make a judgement as to who their leaders might be and the form of their government and the policies of their nation.

Rhodesia is one of those countries—Namibia is another. And the national leaders who hope to lead the new nation of Zimbabwe in the future look to our guest for counsel and for guidance and for support and for leadership and for inspiration.

He has joined with others for many years in struggling for a peaceful solution to the problems in Zimbabwe and Namibia. That has not yet been successful. And I think that it is accurate to say that he and other Front Line Presidents and some of the leaders of the Western democracies in Europe and in our continent, if we are able to work in concert and strive for justice and fairness, might very well bring a peaceful resolution to these questions in the southern part of Africa.

That is my hope and my prayer and I believe that this is the desire of the world.

Our nation is blessed with great individual riches. The people in President Nyerere's country are relatively poor in material things, but they are blessed with a leader and officials of the government who are stable and respected and beloved and justifiably so by the people whom they lead.

We are honoured at your presence, Mr. President, and I would like to propose a toast to the free and independent and light-hearted and hopeful people of your great country and to you, one of the leaders of the world.

In reply Mwalimu says:

Mr. President, this is the second occasion that I have listened to you talk about myself and my country and on both occasions I feel a lump coming here. And then I feel, well, my notes are prepared, so I think the lump will go down.

I do want to thank you very much, Mr. President, for the encouraging words you have been saying about myself and my country both this morning and now.

I have recently been reading some very good books about President Washington and his time, and I have come to the conclusion that the problems of young countries can be very similar.

Although your nation came into existence some two hundred years ago, I suspect that if the first President of your country returned to earth now, he might find it easier to understand the problems of Tanzania better than he understands the problems that you face in the United States.

I suspect he might even be able to understand better my one-party system than your multi-party system.

For coming from Tanzania in 1977, I am very conscious of a few facts: your country is now 201 years old. It is a firmly established system, strong enough to withstand political crises of great intensity and which cannot be upset by the intrigues or manoeuvres of any other country.

The United Republic of Tanzania became independent less than sixteen years ago—our union is just thirteen years old, and we replaced our interim constitution only two months ago.

And not less relevant, in area Tanzania is one-tenth the size of the United States—its population is less than one-thirteenth of your population—and the national income of Tanzania is a minute fraction of the national income of your country.

These facts, Mr. President, must affect the relationship between our two countries, and at least Tanzania's attitude towards your country.

If you don't mind me saying it: where the law of the jungle still reigns, the pygmies are very wary of the giants.

For questions of world peace and justice do affect both our countries regardless of our differences in size. But your country is not only concerned about the problems of maintaining peace and building justice everywhere as my country is.

The great size and strength of your country and its economic power mean that the United States is also directly or indirectly involved in these matters everywhere in the world. It is therefore not strange that in the United States and in our discussions I should be concerned to learn more about your ideas and policies towards Africa. Nor is it suprising that I welcome the opportunity to explain to you and to your colleagues our commitment to the liberation of southern Africa from colonialism and racialism and our ideas about how this can be brought about.

Yet although the situation in southern Africa is simple in principle, it is not a simple one in practice. To achieve the liberation of Africa, we have to bring to an end the political, economic and military structures in Rhodesia, in Namibia and South Africa which are of long-standing and great, although varying, strength.

These structures will sooner or later be changed. The forces of nationalism cannot be defeated in the long run, and men will never willingly accept deliberate and organized humiliation as the price of existence.

But how, and how quickly, these changes can be brought about is a vital concern to all the peoples of these areas, both black and white, to the rest of Africa and also to the rest of the world.

It is unlikely that Tanzania and your country, Mr. President, will agree on all aspects of how and how quickly some of these changes will be able to be brought about in southern Africa.

The problem of southern Africa has an urgency and a priority to Tanzania which this country may not share, but I believe that our two governments will not on this issue again find themselves working for different objectives.

I think we shall also find some points of agreement on how to assist the necessary changes.

We in Tanzania have noticed with great pleasure the emphasis which you, Mr. President, and your colleagues, give to support human rights in the world. We welcome this emphasis.

I am well aware as you yourself have said about America—no country warrants a clean report on this matter of human rights. Certainly Tanzania does not. No one in this country could be more aware of our faults than I am myself. But I do believe it to be important that this powerful country whose founding fathers gave to the world that immortal liberation manifesto, the American Declaration of Independence, is now allowing this concern for human rights to influence its policies on major world issues and its relations with other countries in the world.

You have also said, Mr. President, that questions of human rights cannot be the only factor affecting America's relations with others, especially when the security of the United States is concerned. In saying that, you were, it seems to me, just being honest and open with the people who elected you, for there is a realism in action for practising politicians but which philosophers and others without responsibility can evade. This is also, unfortunately, the kind of realism which can lead to differences between statesmen who share the same broad political goals.

In the case of southern Africa, however, we believe that the long-term interests of the United States lie in the rapid end of racialism and colonialism in southern Africa. In particular, the United States is now struggling to rectify the bitter effects of centuries of racial inequality and discrimination in your own country.

I do not believe this struggle within your country would be made easier by the continued racial insult of apartheid in South Africa and the institutionalized racial domination in Rhodesia.

We have been greatly impressed and encouraged by what you, Mr. President, and your colleagues—the Vice President, the Secretary of State and your Ambassador to the United Nations—have been saying about these matters. And now I have had a chance to exchange views with you and I am greatly impressed and greatly encouraged—for in the past, American power has been an impediment to Africa's liberation. Now we feel that your power can be an aid to our struggle.

Your coming to the White House, Mr. President, has not changed the international law of the jungle, but our apprehensions have been greatly reduced by your coming to the White House.

Mr. President, our two countries are also mutually involved in other issues, especially matters relating to the international economic system, the law of the sea and general relations between the rich and the poor nations of this world. On these and similar subjects the differences in our power and wealth and our different approach to questions of production and distribution may continue to keep our representatives on different sides at the relevant international conferences. I do not pretend that these matters are small matters—malnutrition and preventable disease, ignorance and the lack of any resources with which to fight these evils are very fundamental to those personally affected.

But even in this area, it may be that we can extend our points of agreement a little, and I do believe that greater mutual understanding can flow from discussion on these topics also, and that this will be promoted by the goodwill which you and your colleagues have shown to me and my colleagues and which we in Tanzania feel towards you, Mr. President, and the people of your country.

And now, friends, I also ask you to stand up and join me in a toast to President Carter and to the people of the United States.

Nyerere's reply so vividly fascinates his host that at the end Carter rises to speak again, and requests Nyerere to answer questions from the dinner guests. These include government leaders, congressmen and women and leaders of the American community generally. This is just the kind of thing Nyerere wanted. For it gives both sides the opportunity to further clarify issues.

THREE

The morning of 5 August is the second day of the Nyerere/Carter talks. But it begins with Nyerere addressing the first in a series of news conferences during the tour.

PRESS: Mr. President, is there still a possibility of achieving a peaceful transition of power to majority rule in Rhodesia and if so, what is its requirements?

PRESIDENT: The short answer is no. There is no possibility now of achieving majority rule in Rhodesia peacefully. That was possible in 1973/1974, even in 1975; we (President Kaunda and myself) tried very hard. We even spoke to South African officials. We don't usually speak to South African officials but we were so keen to try and see if a negotiated settlement was possible that we met South African officials. President Kaunda went as far as meeting Vorster; we did not succeed, and when we failed we began training very seriously for an armed struggle. So, there is fighting now in Rhodesia; people are dying. As I am speaking here now people are fighting there, people are dying. So the possibility is no longer whether we can achieve majority rule by peaceful means but whether with the combination of non-miltary pressures we can shorten the war and prevent it from being intensified.

PRESS: Do you foresee a role for an international peace-keeping force in Rhodesia before majority rule?

PRESIDENT: I don't know about an international peace-keeping force. There is now fighting taking place in that country. At one time there was a possibility that majority rule would have come about in Rhodesia as a result of an ordinary constitutional process. If majority rule would have come about as a result of an ordinary constitutional process, a new government would have come in and inherited the power structures which are there at present. The army, the police force, the civil service and so forth. This actually is what we were expecting should happen even as late as last year. This has not taken place. So, now you have a guerrilla army and a Smith army. One of those armies will have to go. We believe it is the Smith army which will have to go. How long it takes we don't know; it might take two years, three years or four years. So, when we talk about a peace-keeping force—what is peace-keeping? The British are the colonial power—they could come in and say Smith is a usurper, he should not be there. They could further say, 'If Smith were not there, and we (the British) were there as an ordinary colonial power, we would have carried out the decolonization as we have done in Tanzania, Zambia and other places.'

So the British could come if they want to and remove Smith and his structures. And then begin the process of decolonization. If that is what you mean by a peace-keeping force, fine! If the British come in with their own force, fine! If they come in with a Commonwealth force, fine! But the purpose is to get rid of Smith and his power structure and begin the process of decolonization in co-operation with Nationalist Leaders.

PRESS: Do you really believe that the United States and Britain will apply pressure (a) on Rhodesia and (b) on Namibia?

PRESIDENT: I don't look at the efforts of the British government and the American government as efforts by the people who don't know the truth. They know the truth. They know fighting is taking place. So, I am assuming that their efforts are intended to achieve what I said in my answer to the first question. They are intended to be a combination of pressures on Smith so that you shorten the war and avoid the war being intensified. So, I do welcome the efforts of the British government and the American government for the purpose. We can defeat Smith alone without the support of the British and without the support of the Americans. We did defeat the Portuguese without support of the British and without the support of the Americans. We can do it but it is better if we can get the support of the British and the Americans because this would shorten the process. So this is not either/or. At present there is no either/or, at present we are simply hoping that both the Americans and the British can apply their own pressures and a combination of our guerrilla pressures and their pressures can shorten the war. That I think is the answer to your first question.

On Namibia, again we welcome the efforts of the five to convince the South Africans that they should pull out. In the case of Rhodesia the armed struggle is more advanced than it is in Namibia, but if no movement is made SWAPO and the Organization of African Unity will have no choice except to intensify the armed struggle there. So we are hoping that the efforts of the five will convince the South Africans that change should take place and take place rapidly.

PRESS: Do you and the Nationalists accept the Anglo-American settlement proposals?

PRESIDENT: Well, in the first place I wish I knew them in detail. I would be less than frank if I told you I knew in detail what the proposals of the British and the Americans are; I don't know them! But as I understand it we don't differ on the principles. I think, both the Americans and the British now feel if there is going to be a settlement there you need a constitution and elections on the basis of one-man-one-vote. One time I was quarrelling with the British about 'NIBMAR'—No Independence Before Majority Rule. We wanted the British to assure us that they would not grant independence to Rhodesia except on that basis. The British were not accepting it. Today both the British and the Americans are saying that independence in Rhodesia should be on the basis of one-man-one-vote; fine! I do welcome this. So when the details come out and they are about a constitution on the basis of one-man-one-vote and getting rid of Smith, some kind of interim position which enabled election to take place on the basis of one-man-one-vote, I see no reason why the Nationalists and their friends should not be able to look at them.

PRESS: Mr. President, there are reports that you have a large number of political detainees in your country. Do you care to comment?

PRESIDENT: At my political detainees! At one time there were 3,000. I heard this morning they have gone up to 5,000; that may be another 2,000 since I left Tanzania—before I go back to Tanzania they might be 10,000! We do have political detainees in Tanzania, depending upon your definition of political detainees. If by political detainees you mean politicians or individuals who are now locked up somewhere because they are opposed to the system, I have a few locked up in Tanzania because they are opposed to the system. And I think it is better that they should rest elsewhere and give us an opportunity to see whether we can build a bit of Ujamaa. I have a few. I think I have about four on the mainland. After the assassination of the Vice-President, Karume (he was not assassinated by some people from Mars—he was assassinated by people from Tanzania) we suspected some people. And those you can say organized the assassination because they were opposed to the system. And irrespective of whether you like the system or not, they did assassinate, and so we rounded them up. The trial has taken a long time, we still have them. I am told, together with the four on the mainland, we have about seventeen. Those are political prisoners.

I have a few more. We are the headquarters of the Liberation Committee of the O.A.U. I have some detainees for SWAPO; I have some detainees for ZANU. These fellows don't have governments—they get into trouble and they say, 'What are we going to do with these people?' You say, 'You can't try them on our land, wait until your country becomes independent. In the meantime if they are a problem to your Liberation Movement, I can keep them for you.' So, I have them. And those are political detainees. But they are not 3,000!

But politically it doesn't matter whether you have 3,000 or only three. The answer for political prisoners is as embarrassing for 3,000 as for three! So, I have not told you something with pride. I am only saying this silly idea that I have 3,000 political detainees, is nonsense; but I wish I didn't even have three!

PRESS: Is it not true that by investing in South Africa you expand the economy and thereby afford jobs for more Blacks?

PRESIDENT: When governments go out and invite investments to their countries, they want to strengthen their own economies. So, if the Cubans came here and sought for investment from here, I don't know whether you would say yes, we should invest in Cuba; we should help the Cubans. Because this will naturally help the government of Cuba to strengthen its position. When you invest in South Africa you strengthen the government of South Africa. You make it stronger. You make it more capable of carrying out its policies.

When you receive the dividends from that system, whatever you may say, you are reaping the dividends of apartheid—no doubt at all. When the dividends are very good you say, 'Thank you very much, sir; that definitely is a very good place to invest. They give us very good dividends.' Why? Because they pay very small wages to the Blacks there. So you thank God or Vorster for apartheid. Investments in southern Africa cannot help the oppressed; they help the oppressor. People here know it. They don't invest in the Soviet Union. They wouldn't pour in money in the Soviet Union in order to help those people in the Soviet Union who are complaining about their system. You know it, people here know it. But you know the human mind is such, they say South Africa is different. So pour money into South Africa—but you are pouring money into South Africa to help Vorster. Do you know that when your people here were fighting the Germans, Vorster was in detention? He was a supporter of Hitler. He was locked up. That Vorster now is a liberal! !

PRESS: Did you get the impression that President Carter understood your position?

PRESIDENT: Yes, I found in President Carter an understanding of the problems. He knows we are fighting. I didn't find that he thinks we are fighting in order to hand over Zimbabwe to the communist countries which are giving her arms. I think he understands why we have to fight for independence. I found that he understands the need for the Western world to apply pressures to bring about majority rule in southern Africa and therefore shorten these wars. I felt very encouraged after talking to him. What will actually happen I do not know, but I feel here you have a President who has power; who given the Americans' support, could put that power behind the liberation movements in Africa.

PRESS: So you found the Carter administration better than the Ford administration?

PRESIDENT: I do not want to get involved in local politics. There used to be administrations in the past which appeared to accept South Africa's definition of a communist, which is anybody who accepts any of the aims of communism. It did happen that these communists also accept that we should achieve our independence. So as a result we were communists. We got the impression that people in this country including people in high position sometimes accepted that definition.

I find that the present administration doesn't believe that those who are forced to take up arms in order to fight for the independence of their own country are necessarily communists. I think there is a realization here that although in 1776 there were no communists on the scene, the urge for independence still remains the same. And if you were helped by the French it is not because you wanted to be French. If we are helped by the Russians or the Chinese it is not because we want to be Russians or Chinese. We need this help for an objective which is accepted by everybody. And I find there is a kind of understanding now in the United States. You are so powerful that even that understanding alone is an encouragement.

PRESS: Andy Young is reported to have been pushing for the freedom fighters to lay down their arms and engage in talks instead.

PRESIDENT: I am saying in southern Africa we are fighting and I am not aware that Andy Young was suggesting to the liberation forces that they should lay down their arms. I have never heard him saying, 'Lay down your arms and we rely upon talking.' I am not aware of him saying that. I am sure a number of people in southern Africa, including myself, would be saying 'Andy Young you are not being too serious.' But I am not aware if he said that.

But there is no doubt that if there is a possibility of achieving your objectives through non-violent means, you do it. People dying is not a matter of sacrament; you don't die because you want to go to heaven. People want to live in peace. It is in desperation that they decide that some of them should die in order that others may live in freedom. We have been forced to take arms but if a combination of guerrilla fighting and non-violent pressures can shorten the war, we welcome that. Therefore, I would say, if that is what Andy Young is saying, I would say yes, I agree with him. If somebody is saying, 'No, forget talking now. Since you can't get arms from Washington, don't even seek any other pressures from Washington. 'I would say, 'You are not serious because Washington has pressures on these countries and if they can use their pressures this would shorten the war.'

PRESS: What pressures can this country apply on southern Africa?

PRESIDENT: Many. You can stop investing in southern Africa. That is not a war, but we can weaken those racialist regimes there. That is possible. United Nations has applied sanctions against Rhodesia. At one time your own country here was breaking those sanctions. The new administration has since restored some of the sanctions. But I am sure there are many leakages yet to the sanctions. Your country has the ability, together with other western countries, to seal some of those leakages to the sanctions. There are many things that can be done. Whenever we go to the United Nations and urge the isolation of South Africa as a country that has inhuman policies, United States use their power to veto us. You can stop using that veto to give encouragement to that regime. These are the kind of pressures, I am sure, western countries could apply. They support that regime.

PRESS: Is it your view that Smith will accept the Anglo-American proposals?

PRESIDENT: Some people have believed that Smith can be argued into accepting majority rule. This is not so. Smith can't be argued into accepting majority rule; he has to be forced. And I am here to find out what kind of force I can get from Washington.

I get arms from the Soviet Union, and I get arms from China. I want to find out what kind of force I can get from here; I don't expect to get arms at all from here. But I want to say this: that we will fight to the end. We defeated the Portuguese without any assistance from the western world. We can defeat Smith and his friends without any assistance from the western world. But I hope we can get some assistance from the western world and if we get it I will welcome it. But we can defeat them without any asistance from the western world.

PRESS: If the United States fails to give you the kind of pressures you are looking for, what effect would that have on relations between your country and ours?

PRESIDENT: You did not help us in the case of the Portuguese, and here I am, we have good diplomatic relations!

'If I get support from the United States to bring about majority rule in southern Africa, would I still be able to control the destiny of my own country?—is this the question?'

PRESS: That is the question.

PRESIDENT: There are many people in this country and in Western Europe who believe that when we take arms from the Soviet Union or from China, because those are the only countries which give us arms to use in the liberation struggle, we shall be controlled. We shall not be in a position to control the destinies of our own countries because we have accepted arms from the Soviet Union. Well, I am still in control of my situation and I have received a lot of arms for the liberation movements from the communist countries.

If you can persuade your country to give me arms, and you have some very good arms here, I will take them with gratitude. I will give them to the liberation movements. We will train them and we will use them to achieve our own independence. If you think, then, as a result of that you are going to run Tanzania, you'll make a big mistake.

PRESS: The majority of Smith's army is Black?

PRESIDENT: When you fought the British here, did you have loyalists? Americans were fighting on the side of the British!

PRESS: Why haven't you defeated them?

PRESIDENT: But we will defeat them.

PRESS: You will, but for how long have you been fighting?

PRESIDENT: We have been fighting him for less than two years. Give us a little more time.

PRESS: Did you feel that President Carter is committed to assisting you to find a solution to the problems of southern Africa?

PRESIDENT: How would I answer this question! Have I not answered this question?

PRESS: You have, but you haven't answered it clearly.

PRESIDENT: What is clearly? Now you frame it in such a manner that I can answer it clearly. I want American power to be put on the side of the liberation struggle in southern Africa. As a result of the talks I have had with President Carter I feel there is a willingness in this administration to put at least some of that power behind the liberation movement in southern Africa. Don't ask me exactly how that power is going to be used because I am not President Carter. But I feel encouraged.

PRESS: What about South Africa itself?

PRESIDENT: I am concentrating on Namibia and Rhodesia for the time being.

PRESS: Did the British and American negotiators really hold Smith's feet to the fire good enough?

PRESIDENT: What is this expression, hold Smith's feet to the fire?

PRESS: I mean did they apply the screws fully?

PRESIDENT: I have a feeling that they did not screw him enough!

PRESS: What assistance are you seeking and getting from other sources?

PRESIDENT: We seek assistance from everybody. For instance, during our struggle in the Portuguese colonies the Scandinavians did not give us arms but they supported us. They gave money, they gave us moral support. And now the small countries of Western Europe, Scandinavian countries and now Holland, give us tremendous support. They don't give us arms but they give us money on condition we don't buy arms; but we can buy quinine!

PRESS: Your country is not exactly a Front Line State. Are you here then just to listen to what President Carter has to say and then pass it over to your colleagues?

PRESIDENT: I am involved. I train freedom fighters. I couldn't possibly be just a listener. I try to explain what the problems are as I see them. I seek assistance. I am here. My colleagues of the Front Line States are not here but I am here. I am trying to find out from President Carter; and in London I may find out from the British what exactly they are proposing. My colleagues will say, 'What did you find out?' I will say, 'I found something which perhaps is worth listening to.' That's what I am here for. In the meantime the training goes on.

At the end of the news conference, Nyerere proceeds once again to the White House, for that second round of talks on southern Africa.

On Namibia, Nyerere seeks American pressure on the South African regime to relinquish its illegal occupation. As was the case in the talks on Rhodesia, the two Presidents reach complete agreement. But their views on the role played by Cuba in helping the people of Angola thwart the South African invasion* of their country are poles apart. They tell each other so and after a lively discussion they settle on disagreeing. But on Namibia America commits herself to continue to spearhead the efforts of the five Western countries on the Security Council* to get South Africa out of Namibia, paving the way for its independence by 1978.

Nyerere knows too well that the understanding and goodwill achieved during the talks with Carter could be seriously hampered by an ill-informed or hostile Congress. Thus Congress itself is his next target later that morning. There, a luncheon has been laid on by the Senate Foreign Relations Committee and the House International Relations Committee. Before the luncheon he has the opportunity

* South Africa sent massive military personnel into Angola in November 1976, to assist UNITA troops in an effort to prevent the M.P.L.A. from coming to power. In response to this aggression, the M.P.L.A. sought and got Cuban military assistance.

* The United States, The United Kingdom, Canada, the Federal Republic of Germany and France.

of meeting and exchanging views with congressional leaders, several of whom he has met before either in the U.S. or in Tanzania. At toast time he launches his appeal for support and understanding:

Senator Clark, Representative Zablocki, Members of Congress, Friends,

I greatly appreciate this opportunity to have informal discussions with you as friends, and as elected representatives of the American people, and I thank you for your invitation.

Visiting Presidents—or perhaps I should say this visiting President!—have just a few things which they themselves wish to say to their hosts, although it is of course possible that the hosts may have some things which *they* wish to say also! If he is not careful, the visitor is therefore liable even in a few days to sound like an over-used gramophone record!

I have been talking about the urgency of the freedom struggle in southern Africa since five days after Tanganyika's independence. My first official visit to this country in 1963 was in order to discuss southern Africa with the late President Kennedy. It was in 1963 also that I first spoke on an international platform about the dangers to the world of the growing inequalities between rich and poor nations.

Since that time Angola and Mozambique have achieved their independence after a prolonged armed struggle against the Portuguese. And as a result Portugal is also free! But as Rhodesia and Namibia are still colonial territories; as apartheid is now even harsher in South Africa; and as the gap between rich and poor has gone on increasing, it would appear that one has to go on campaigning! As fellow politicians you will not be surprised that a combination of some success and great setbacks makes one campaign even harder!

I think people are now more aware of the dangers inherent in the southern African situation. And I think that most people do now recognize that the issue in that area is one of nationalism and human equality versus colonialism and racialism, not communism versus democracy. Also, what words cannot achieve, the Oil Producers managed by action; there is now a lot of talking about the need to wage war against world poverty! I wish I could say there has been much action, but perhaps the world is leading up to that!

If so, it will need your help as Members of Senate and of the House of Representatives.

Friends, you organized this lunch so that we could exchange ideas, not so that you could listen to me making a speech. But let me just say that we in Tanzania, and I believe in Africa, do appreciate the sympathetic interest in our concerns and our problems which we receive from friends in the Congress—a number of whom I am happy to see here today. It cannot always be easy for you; the people of your different states and constituencies may sometimes have other ideas about how you should be spending your time!

It is with great sincerity, therefore, that I ask you all to join me in a Toast:

To the United States Congress and all its Members;
to President Carter;
and to all the people of the United States of America.

As at the White House dinner the previous night, Nyerere avails himself of this opportunity to answer questions from the congressmen and women.

At Howard University later that afternoon, the President speaks on the pressing need to change the present world economic order so as to narrow and finally bridge the growing gap between the world's rich and poor nations.

Nyerere's effort to meet as many influential leaders of U.S. opinion as possible to press home his case for southern Africa, benefit further that evening through a reception organized by Tanzania's Ambassador, Paul Bomani. There are no speeches here. But the President is able to meet, shake hands and chat with a wide cross-section of the American people.

FOUR

Nyerere's two days in official Washington have received a wide coverage in the electronic media and the press. *Washington Post's* correspondent Jacqueline Trescott, sees Nyerere's as a calm voice from a tense continent. She writes:

As the limousine of Julius Nyerere made its way through the White House gates on Thursday evening, a passing tourist asked the guard who the passenger was.

The guard, overheard by a Capitol Hill aide, replied, 'It's the President of Tanzania, wherever that is.'

Where Tanzania is, bordering on some of the most explosive southern African states, and who Julius Nyerere is, Africa's leading intellectual, are two of the reasons why his two-day visit to Washington this week has been so wrapped up in work, and minus the trappings of the usual state visit.

Nyerere, the leader of Tanzania since before its indepedence in 1961, is a man of spartan tastes and serious manner. So he seemed to enjoy the carousel of conferences and whirl of questions.

'Do you think that there will be a peaceful transition of power in Rhodesia, sir?'

Nyerere was seated on a red couch, a foot or two behind the microphones, as he started to answer the first question of the press conference. 'Stand up, stand up, we can't hear you,' someone shouted. 'Oh, I should answer this question standing up?' Nyerere replied, his small face ballooning into a smile. He seemed amused at the insistence of the press, its intensity, but understood the necessity of their catching his every word. He looked glum as he said, 'The short answer is no.'

It is the short and the long answers that Jimmy Carter, and his foreign policy advisers, want to hear. It was both practical and ironic that Julius Nyerere was the first African head of state invited by Carter.

As spokesman for the nations that border the white-ruled countries of southern Africa, Nyerere has been a key negotiator (with Zambia's President Kenneth Kaunda) between American and British initiatives, especially in Rhodesia, and black political leaders.

But his prestige extends far beyond those borders. In the last few months Nikolai Podgorny (then President of the Soviet Union), Cuban President Fidel Castro, British Foreign Secretary David Owen and U.S. Ambassador to the United Nations Andrew Young had audiences with Nyerere in Dar es Salaam.

Yet, for many years his relations with the United States were cool, primarily because his economic building programmes and political philosophy for Tanzania were based on an African socialism, not capitalism. The West saw red for many years. As the

United States began to shape a dormant African policy into a major concern in the past year, Nyerere has moved into its circle of counsellors.

In Tanzania he is known as the Mwalimu, the teacher. When Nyerere expounded on the role of South Africa in southern Africa at the working dinner at the White House on Thursday, Carter took notes for the first time during the evening.

Responding to a question by representative Charles Diggs,* Chairman of the Africa sub-committee of the House Committee on Foreign Affairs, Nyerere never raised his voice as he explained how the concept of apartheid must be changed, even if initially through the enfranchisement of the Indians and the coloureds. 'That would be a break in the dam,' said Nyerere.

'Do you think the American and British negotiators really held Smith's feet to the fire good enough?' asked Marilyn Robinson of N.B.C. News.

'What is this expression, "hold Smith's feet to the fire?" ' asked Nyerere. 'Well, did they apply the screws fully on him?' Robinson pressed. 'I have a feeling they did not screw him enough,' said Nyerere with a laugh.

Twice yesterday they lined up to meet him, diplomat shoulder-to-shoulder with gym teacher, diamond importer shoulder-to shoulder with priest. It was not only the heads of state who sought out this sparely built man, with the snowy head of hair and the brown eyes that bulged when he made a point.

At Howard University, where Nyerere made a major speech, people who had come from as far as Indiana were turned away. At a reception at the Capital Hilton last night the well-known had to jostle with the plain folks.

Henry Kissinger, who as Secretary of State had been uncomfortably put on the defensive by Nyerere in Africa last fall, showed no hard feelings. They embraced. 'He was a worthy opponent,' said Kissinger as he walked away, then corrected quickly, 'We were working on the same problems and I told him they haven't changed.'

Despite a circle of Secret Service men holding hands around him, the jostling crowds forced Nyerere to move from the main reception room at the Capital Hilton to a smaller one across the hall. The crowd followed.

---

* (Democrat-Michigan)

Han Hsu, the Deputy Chief of the People's Republic of China's liaison office, the man who had been Chief of Protocol when Chou en-Lai visited Tanzania, made it through, as did Max Robinson, the television anchorman and his wife Beverly, writer Quincy Troupe and others. But the many who didn't get to shake Nyerere's hand were disappointed and disgruntled.

Verta Mae Grosvenor, a New York based writer, said several other artists, besides herself, were annoyed at the arrangements. 'It's just a shame. People put a lot of money into travelling and they don't get to meet this great man,' she said.

In the end, there was some satisfaction just being in the presence of a man like Nyerere. And when he left the two-hour reception, those in the hall shouted, 'Kwa heri,' good-bye in Swahili.

Walter Washington and Douglas Moore hopped into Blair House on Thursday to give the keys to the city to Nyerere. Moore, a city councilman who has lived in Africa and knows the continent's languages, upstaged the mayor. 'I was going to do it in Swahili,' said Moore, 'but the language is not the same in Tanzania as in Zaire.' Nyerere said, very quietly, 'It's still Swahili.' 'Why don't you just do it in English?' Washington said, rather sternly. They told Nyerere that the D.C. City Council had declared Saturday Julius Nyerere day. And at the end of their conversation Moore managed to get in some Swahili, saying, 'I want to thank you' or 'Nanina taka kusema' (sic).

It is said that Nyerere cannot be bought. He does not like compromise. 'If I protect Africa for anybody, it will be to protect it for Africa,' said Nyerere at a luncheon with several Senators yesterday. Coming out of the luncheon, his first meeting with the Tanzanian President, Sen. George McGovern,* said he admired his authority. 'He's as impressive as any head of state we have had here,' said McGovern.

Ujamaa! Ujamaa! (Familyhood) Uhuru! Uhuru! (Freedom) Mwalimu! Mwalimu! (teacher). As soon as Nyerere stepped in view of the audience at Howard University yesterday, the shouts rang out. Nyerere smiled warmly and motioned the audience to sit down.

Yet, in his speech in front of the predominantly black audience that filled two auditoriums, Nyerere did not once mention the

* Democrat, South Dakota.

hot spots—Rhodesia, South Africa or Namibia. Instead he spoke of the economic struggle of poor people. 'Our poverty has not arisen from our actions or inactions in Tanzania,' said Nyerere, moving back and forth on his toes. 'The poor should not find themselves trying to run up the down escalator while the rich go sailing upward.'

FIVE

Saturday, 6 August, Nyerere is off to the Midwest and Western United States. There he is to meet more American people and their leaders and members of the business community. But before he sets off he has his first network television interview, on American Broadcasting Company's *Issues and Answers.*

PRESS: You came to Washington seeking the support of President Carter and the American people in the struggle for black liberation in southern Africa—liberation from white rule.

Did you receive the assurances you hoped for from President Carter? Did he promise you political or economic support in the efforts to achieve black majority rule in Rhodesia and other parts of southern Africa?

PRESIDENT: I think I can say yes. I wanted basically two things.

First, I wanted to be sure that there is a President now in the White House who no longer believes that those who are forced to take up arms to fight for the independence of their own countries in southern Africa are communists, simply because it is only the communists who are willing to give them arms.

I have got that confirmation. As a matter of fact, I think at the White House the President said to me, 'Your country, Mr. President, achieved independence without fighting. We achieved our independence after taking up arms and fighting.'

That is one thing. It is completely different.

I discovered that the President is not making a show about majority rule. He is not trying to please us about majority rule. He is committed to the achievement of majority rule in southern Africa.

Secondly, I found that he is willing—I can't say what pressures what actual pressures he is going to use to bring about majority rule in southern Africa, but I found that he is willing, together with his allies in Western Europe, to put on whatever pressures are needed in order to bring about majority rule, so I feel very encouraged.

PRESS: We want to talk more about those pressures later, but you told reporters after your first meeting with President Carter that it is too late for any peaceful transition to black majority rule in Rhodesia; in effect, there is no way to compromise with Ian Smith on giving the vote to Blacks in Rhodesia. Were you that pessimistic with the President or did you give him some more hopeful view?

PRESIDENT: I don't know whether I am being pessimistic or anything. I am simply stating a fact that at present fighting is taking place in Rhodesia. The Smith army and the guerrilla armies are engaged in a war; the Smith army, from time to time, crosses the border and causes a lot of trouble in Mozambique. More Mozambicans are dying in this war of liberation for Zimbabwe than died in their own war of liberation for Mozambique. So the war is there.

What we are trying to get Western countries to help us in this war is to use diplomatic pressures rather than guerrilla pressures; it is the combination of the Western and non-military pressures which, together with the guerrilla fighting which is taking place now, can shorten the war.

What we really want is the shortening of the war. It is no longer either/or. Either/or was around '74, even as late as '75. It was possible to achieve independence in Rhodesia without fighting. Now fighting is taking place.

What we are trying to do is to see how much Western pressure we can mobilize in order that the war can be shortened.

PRESS: Is the war being accelerated, Mr. President, at this point?

PRESIDENT: We must accelerate the war. We are no longer going to say we will de-escalate the war, hoping that by de-escalation Smith is going to be reasonable. We can't do this.

Frankly, we have to escalate the war and we hope then by escalating the war and if President Carter and his allies can escalate their own pressures, these two escalations will shorten the struggle.

PRESS: You mentioned pressures you would hope the Western countries would bring to bear. Did you suggest pressures to President Carter that you feel might be appropriate?

PRESIDENT: Some I did, some I did not. The United Nations applied the economic sanctions against Rhodesia. We all did this in the belief it would help in bringing down the Smith regime as quickly as possible. Two countries did not back up these sanctions. One was Portugal, the other one was South Africa.

Portugal is no longer there. The guerrilla fighting got Portugal out of the way. Now Mozambique applies sanctions. South Africa still refuses to apply sanctions. We are hoping two things: one, that through pressures from the United States and Western allies, South Africa can be pressurized into stopping help for Rhodesia.

Secondly, we hope—I think it is well known that there are leakages in the sanctions carried out by other countries, including the Western countries, and it is possible—the Western countries know it—it is possible to seal those leakages and it is this kind of thing we should do that can help.

PRESS: Prime Minister Ian Smith of Rhodesia, Mr. President, as you know very well, has called a general election in his country at the end of this month where he will seek a mandate from moderate Whites to bring more Blacks into the government. Why not give him this one last chance, if there is any realistic chance of averting the racial war that many fear in Rhodesia?

PRESIDENT: Rhodesia has a peculiar system. They are always moving to the right and when there is trouble the more reactionaries take over. So now there are other reactionaries who want to take over from Smith and because of this contrast, tougher people, more racist than Smith, want to take over.

Smith is being portrayed to us now as a moderate. Now Smith is the moderate who wants majority rule and true negotiations and his right wing reactionaries don't want majority rule.

Well, this is nonsense. Smith is a reactionary. Smith is the one who all the time, all these thirteen years, has stood against any negotiated settlement at all, even without one man, one vote. As late as '74/'75 — I personally was urging the Nationalist leaders to accept a limited franchise as long as it was liberal enough to give Africans sufficient numbers on the roll to get majority rule. I was doing this. It is Smith who rejected this and Smith will continue rejecting this, whatever he says.

I think he has been told by the Americans and the British that they are determined to have one man, one vote, and he wants some method of stopping this. He is not going to succeed.

PRESS: Some moderate black leaders in Rhodesia appear to have very strong support from Blacks there who are concerned about the effect civil war could create. Might it save bloodshed to give these moderate black leaders a final chance to work out an internal solution instead of giving all of your support, the support of the so-called Front Line Countries, to the more radical leaders commanding the guerrilla forces outside the country?

PRESIDENT: The point that really has to be made very clear is that fighting is taking place and those like myself who believe that Smith has necessitated this fighting are saying therefore the fighters have to be supported. To support the fighters, we have to support the Patriotic Front because they are the ones who have the fighters.

To support the negotiations I support Carter, and the Patriotic Front because they have the fighters. I am supporting Carter because he has other pressures he can apply. Both of them, I am hoping, will get us to a position when elections are possible.

When those elections do take place, I am not going to be the one to determine who is going to be elected by the people of Zimbabwe to lead them. I don't think they will necessarily elect Carter because he helped them; I don't think they will vote for him, and they will not necessarily vote for Joshua Nkomo or Robert Mugabe. They are helping, they have the arms, but they will not necessarily vote for them.

PRESS: You would be quite happy, for instance, if they voted for Bishop Muzorewa?

PRESIDENT: Absolutely. It is our only intention that we help the Rhodesians to build an army for Zimbabwe. We are not helping them to build an army for Joshua or for Mugabe or for the Bishop, or for Sithole.

As a matter of fact, when the Nationalists have tried to persuade us to build armies for the factions, we have rejected this.

PRESS: Your position seems to have hardened, Mr. President, since we last talked last September. Is it because the Nationalists have intensified pressure that would appear to have hardened your position?

PRESIDENT: I don't know in what respect my position has hardened. When I believed that negotiations, even on their own, could bring about majority rule, I urged negotiations. I have spoken to South Africans. I have sat down with South African officials. I have sat down with Rhodesian officials, explaining to them what the objectives are. President Kaunda has gone as far as talking to Voster, so whenever we have believed that it is possible to achieve the objective without firing one bullet, we have encouraged this. If we have failed, it is because Smith has been successful.

PRESS: Mr. President, earlier you indicated that perhaps you did make some suggestions to President Carter how the United States might apply pressure in Rhodesia and South Africa. Are you disturbed about the rather substantial American business investments in those countries and did you discuss that with the President?

PRESIDENT: I am disturbed about Western investments in South Africa. The South African regime is really an inhuman regime; it is a peculiar regime; there is no other regime like it in the world. In all our countries, in your country, in my country, we have people who have racial prejudices. We have them here; I have them in Tanzania. The state itself legislates in order to abolish racial discrimination and carries out an intention to end racial prejudices. This is what happens in all our countries.

There is only one country in the world where racial superiority, racial discrimination, is a creed, is a principle of the government of the country, and it is South Africa, and really we should, all of us, you here, we ourselves in Africa and in Western Europe who believe in the equality of human beings, isolate that regime out of the international community until they accept the equality of human beings. They don't.

Now, you don't—your investors treat South Africa as any other country. It is very nice to invest money there and you get good dividends and so you use the dividends of racialism and you pay for racialism, and racialism pays you. You enjoy racialism, and it is good money because they don't pay the wages to the Blacks which they pay to the Whites and, as a result, therefore, if you invest money in South Africa you can get very

A heart to heart exchange

Mrs. Rosalyn Carter chatting with Nyerere

Smiling President Carter listens attentively as President Nyerere speaks at the White House working dinner

Making a point to Sen. Edward Kennedy

Nyerere with Sen. Dick Clark, Chairman, Africa Sub-Committee of the Senate Foreign Relations Committee

Nyerere with Mr. Martti Ahtisaari, U.N. Commissioner for Namibia

The second day of the official talks at the White House

Addressing a press conference at Blair House

Nyerere speaking after receiving an honorary degree of Doctor of Humanities at Howard University, Washington

At the reception in Washington, Nyerere is mobbed by admirers as he slowly takes the rounds, shaking hands

Actor Sidney Poitier with his wife chatting with Nyerere at a Los Angeles, California, reception hosted by Afro-American show-business celebrities

Mayor and Mrs. Tom Bradley at their mansion in Los Angeles, where they hosted a dinner for Nyerere

The dinner guests at Tennessee Governor Blanton's residence

Singer Charlie Pride, after performing for Nyerere and his Party at Opry–band, Nashville. Tennessee Governor Ray Blanton is at the centre

The Atlanta dinner speech, Georgia

Mrs. Corretta King talking to Nyerere after he had visited her husband's grave in Atlanta, Georgia

good dividends, but you are paying for apartheid and you are paid by apartheid to invest. I did not discuss this with President Carter, but this is my belief.

PRESS: And Mr. President, the United States and Britain have called an informal conference of some sort in London this week to discuss South African problems. Among those present will be Foreign Minister Botha of South Africa. There have been reports that you will attend that meeting or at least that you have been urged to attend, since you will be passing through London. Will you be there?

PRESIDENT: I think the President may have been misunderstood on what he said. He told me there is going to be a meeting in London between your Secretary of State and the British, and Botha is going to be there and he wondered if on my passing through London, your Secretary of State could brief me on whatever they may have discussed. I think that is what he said and they thought I was going to join their conference. If I join a conference with them and Botha, I don't know whether I will receive a very good welcome when I go back home.

PRESS: You have said, Mr. President, that your country, Tanzania, would not commit troops to the fighting in Rhodesia. You are giving support to the insurgent forces, but you have also predicted if the casualities among Whites in Rhodesia got too high, that Whites in South Africa would bring pressure on their government to enter the fighting in Rhodesia. If the conflict did broaden to include South Africa, would your country commit troops or take an active military role?

PRESIDENT: The answer to that is yes. It won't really matter very much.

I keep saying to those people, including the French, who arm South Africa, that we are not a military threat to South Africa. Not a single African country is really a military threat to South Africa. No combination of African countries can really be a military threat to South Africa, but as a matter of principle, if the South Africans enter that war, they will endanger not simply the progress of liberation in Zimbabwe itself, they will endanger the security of Zambia and the security of Mozambique and we will choose to hang together rather than hang separately. We will commit our own troops, but this is not the most serious thing.

The most serious thing is that those countries may want to seek military support from countries where that support is not simply symbolic, as my support would be simply symbolic, but where it would be fatal. That is the fear. Besides, the Rhodesians want it because the Rhodesians want to escalate that war, they want to internationalize the war. They, therefore, want to attract the South Africans into this. As I understand it, the South Africans are being hesitant, but if it happens there is not the slightest doubt, I will commit troops. But presently I repeat, it is purely symbolic.

PRESS: Are you suggesting, Mr. President, we are on the verge of an explosion in southern Africa unlike anything that has happened in the past?

PRESIDENT: I am not saying that. I am saying southern Africa can erupt, there is no doubt. I am still saying, through what I was reading about the policies of your President about southern Africa, through the discussions I have had with him, I believe that we can put the necessary kind of pressures, combined pressures, your pressures, our pressures, to bear on the South Africans with regard to Namibia and Rhodesia and achieve independence quickly.

What is going to happen with regard to South Africa itself, that is a different matter. I don't believe myself that the South Africans—they are the power—they are really the leaders of racialism in southern Africa—I don't believe they will dig in either in Rhodesia or in Namibia. So, given sufficient pressures from us and from your people, I believe we can shorten the wars in those two countries.

In South Africa itself, I can't predict.

PRESS: Mr. President, I want to ask you, because there appear to be some signs that some sort of a trade-off may be developing between Namibia in Southwest Africa and Rhodesia, and I say that because President Carter said this week after his talks with you, if South Africa continues to show what he called a co-operative attitude in working with the United Nations to bring about a free Namibia, the President said, 'I think the threat of additional sanctions against South Africa would be inappropriate now.'

That seems to carry the hint that if there is progress that the South Africans will join us in moving toward freedom in Namibia, then he will not put pressure on them in Rhodesia?

PRESIDENT: I don't know, but I am an optimist and I have been encouraged by President Carter. This is the first time a President in the White House has said, if this does not happen, or implies that if certain things don't happen, sanctions may be applied against South Africa itself. Now this doesn't discourage me. I feel very encouraged. This is the first time a voice from the White House is hinting that unless there is co-operation to bring about change in southern Africa, sanctions may be considered against South Africa itself. I don't want to misinterpret this. I want to interpret it as encouragement to us.

PRESS: Mr. President, it is traditional to include in an interview with you a question about communism in Africa.

White leaders in both Rhodesia and South Africa have made much of the fact that guerrilla forces are supplied with communist arms from both Russia and China. You have often said that Western fears about communist designs in Africa are greatly exaggerated. What, in your view, is the purpose of the communist countries in supplying arms?

PRESIDENT: I think the purpose of the communists in supplying arms would—I don't know—would be similar to the purpose of, say, President Carter in assisting us. I think they want regimes which are friendly to them.

I would be surprised that the Russians would be giving us arms to achieve independence in Angola, in Mozambique, in Zimbabwe, and not expect that when this has been achieved there will be regimes there which are going to be friendly to them.

This is true also of the United States. I believe that President Carter is saying, 'If we want friendship with these countries in southern Africa, let's help them to achieve their ends, to achieve their objectives, hoping that, if that happens, we are going to have regimes in southern Africa which are friendly to the United States.'

Now, whether that actually could happen, I really don't know. I am only saying. I think it is very reasonable, but the idea which I have always rejected, is that if we take arms from the communist countries, then we are not fighting for freedom, we are fighting for the replacement of one master with another; this has never sounded serious to me at all.

Your own country was assisted by the French, but I don't really believe you wanted to get rid of the British so that the French should take over your country.

PRESS: Mr. President, I am sorry to have to stop you here. We are out of time.

Thank you very much for being our guest on *Issues and Answers*.

SIX

The President arrives in San Francisco late in the afternoon and delivers his first major speech on southern Africa to an enthusiastically cheering audience of over two thousand at the Veteran's Memorial Hall. The audience, drawn mainly from the World Affairs Council of the United States, repeatedly interrupts the speech with approving cheers.

Your Excellencies, Ladies and Gentlemen,
Thank you for the kindness of your reception. I am pleased to have this opportunity to meet with you. I propose to talk about our problems in southern Africa.

In 1950 there were three independent states in Africa—Ethiopia, Liberia and South Africa. When I first visited California in February 1960, eleven African countries were independent. In 1977 there are two countries which are not independent—Namibia and Rhodesia. Except in the case of Algeria, Angola, Guinea Bissau and Mozambique, this revolutionary change was achieved by peaceful means.

No one could suggest that African independence has always been followed by personal freedom, justice, and human rights for all the inhabitants of the new states. The horrors which have been committed in some independent African states are a disgrace to Africa and to the world. It is therefore good that other peoples of the world, as well as Africans within Africa, should keep up the pressure on independent African governments to recognize and extend to all their peoples the basic rights of humanity. I have no quarrel with the emphasis which the present American administration gives to this matter. On the contrary, I am glad of it.

But faults or even crimes within newly independent African states do not invalidate the demand for political freedom for Rhodesia and Namibia, or the demand for an end to apartheid in South Africa. Nor do they reduce the justice of the demand that the world should support the struggle against institutionalized racialism in southern Africa. On the contrary, they make it more urgent. For the real struggle for individual human liberation cannot even begin until national liberation has been secured; talk of individual human rights does not make sense while the very humanity of millions of people is denied because of their colour or their ancestry.

Rhodesia is a British colony with an entrenched White minority government which is in rebellion against the Crown. Namibia is a United Nations Trusteeship Territory, illegally occupied by South Africa and governed to a large extent as if it were an integral part of South Africa. Thus, in both cases forces external to Africa have a legal as well as a moral responsibility for the present state of affairs—and its correction. And in both cases, the responsible external authority has declared its commitment to national independence on the basis of majority rule, but explicitly or implicitly denied its power to effect the change. Namibia remains a *de facto* colony of South Africa despite U.N. decisions. Rhodesia continues to be ruled by the 4.4 per cent of its population who are white, despite policies enunciated by the British government and backed up by the U.N. Security Council.

This situation continues because South Africa makes it continue. The problem of Rhodesia and Namibia therefore cannot be considered without reference to South Africa. And although South Africa is legally an independent and sovereign state, its 24 million people are governed by the 4 million who are white, because they are white. South Africa is not only a tyrannical police state, it is also the only country in the world whose government is openly based upon race, and which practises as well as propagates the doctrine of racial supremacy. South Africa is a threat to world peace both because it is upholding racialism and colonialism, and because it challenges the world movement towards human dignity for all.

The three problems of Namibia, Rhodesia, and South Africa

are thus linked. The legal distinctions, as well as the historical and geographical differences between them, are important; they affect the means by which movement towards human equality and self-determination can be achieved. But the principles at stake are similar, if not the same, in all cases.

In South Africa the principle of human equality is denied—by constitution, by law and in practice. The doctrine of apartheid, or racial separation, is the official philosophy of the state, and is enforced upon everyone. Whatever he may himself believe, no South African—of any colour—may act as a non-racialist, a believer in human unity, within that country. If you are white, you are a first-class citizen; you have a vote; freedom to organize politically and in trade unions; you can even criticize the government within the limits it lays down. If you are brown—either with Asian ancestry or because of past unions across the colour-line—the South African state makes you into a second-class citizen; you have no vote, but your racially-fixed wages will be higher than those of Africans. If you are black you are a third-class citizen, with no political rights within the land of your birth, no right to move your residence from one part of the country to another—indeed, no rights at all. In recent years the South African government is even going further; it is trying to pretend that the people of African descent are not South Africans at all.

With minor variations, which are a remnant of the League of Nations Mandate, the same doctrine of racial supremacy is applied in Namibia by the occupying power. Whites vote for representatives in the South African parliament; Africans live in designated tribal areas, or under contract within the Police Zone—which covers over 50 per cent of the land area and is really reserved for use by the 10 percent of the population which is white.

In Rhodesia apartheid is not the official philosophy; the Whites prefer to talk of government by 'civilized men'. The result is not unsimilar; 270,000 white people (about 30 per cent of whom have entered the country since the White minority declared their country independent) have an entrenched majority in government and parliament, as well as dominating the army, police, public service, and the economy. There are almost 6 million black Rhodesians.

Not suprisingly, these political and economic structures are rejected by the majority of the people of those three countries.

There is in every one of them a long history of political protest, of petitions, demonstrations, and appeal for justice. Indeed the African National Congress of South Africa was formed in 1912—ten years before I was born. But all African peaceful agitation has been ruthlessly smashed, while the oppression has got greater. Finally, even the extreme patience of Africans in these areas has been exhausted. For when other means fail, men are so constituted that they are willing to die for freedom. A war is now being waged in Rhodesia; it has begun in Namibia. In South Africa the people of Soweto and other non-white townships (as well as those in the rural areas about whom we hear less), rise in spontaneous revolt.

The demand for political freedom, and for an end to apartheid or other forms of institutionalized racialism, is made by the peoples of Rhodesia, Namibia, and South Africa. Their demand receives the full support of all independent African states. The Freedom Fighters of Rhodesia and Namibia are given full backing by the O.A.U.; the so-called 'Front Line States' help them with training, and by providing a 'rear base' for their operations. We do this because we know that we have no more—and no less—right to govern ourselves than have the people of South Africa, and because apartheid is a continuing threat to our own attempts to build non-racial states.

But African states do not manufacture weapons of war. As the Freedom Fighters cannot battle with bows and arrows against guns, tanks, and aeroplanes, we therefore also provide transit facilities for the arms which the Liberation Forces manage to acquire. And they get all their arms from communist countries, because no other state will make them available. Even countries sympathetic to the freedom cause like Scandinavia and the Netherlands will only supply humanitarian assistance; this is necessary and appreciated, but it does not help to wage the war.

The South African and Rhodesian minorities rejoice at the source of the Freedom Fighters' weapons. They use it as backing for their argument that they are fighting communism and therefore deserve the support of America and other democratic nations. And some Western countries like France accept this argument and help to arm South Africa. But the argument itself is not new. It is made possible because of the peculiar definitions given to 'communism' and 'democracy' in those states. For under South African law, a communist is anyone who supports any of the aims of communism; one of these declared aims is human equality regardless of race. Mr. Vorster and Mr. Smith—and their supporters—sometimes also have the effrontery to say that they are supporters of democracy; at other times they pour scorn on the idea of 'counting noses'. They are able to hold these two contradictory ideas simultaneously in the same way as the American Founding Fathers were able to declare that 'all men are created equal' while upholding slavery. The intervening two hundred years have brought change in U.S.A. We still have a long way to go in southern Africa.

The conflict in southern Africa is not a capitalist versus communist struggle at all. It is a nationalist struggle for political freedom and for human equality. The final result is therefore certain. What is yet to be determined is the means by which nationalism will triumph, the human suffering which will be involved in the struggle, and the extent to which the rest of the world will be militarily involved.

Realizing the dangers to world peace arising out of war in southern Africa, the Western world has urged patience on the victims and tried to scold South Africa and Rhodesia into joining the twentieth century. There is also a particular argument that the way to change apartheid is through political, economic and social contact. It is argued that increased South African prosperity (promoted by foreign investment and trade) will strain the restrictions of apartheid beyond breaking point, while the example of more liberal societies will convince the Whites of South Africa that they have nothing to fear from change.

Policies based on these arguments have been followed since apartheid first became the official doctrine in 1948. They have clearly failed. And that failure was inevitable.

First, if South Africa or Rhodesia or Namibia were governed by the majority of the people, the Whites would lose their economic and social privileges. No South African government responsible to the majority of the people could acquiesce for a moment in 87 per cent of the land area being reserved for White occupation, with the other 13 per cent allocated to the 18 million Black people, while Asians and Coloureds have no right to any form of land ownership anywhere. No government resting upon the will of the people could continue to allocate 28.5 rand for the education of each black school pupil, and over 400 rand for each white pupil—

as in South Africa, or £22 and £249 respectively as is now the case in Rhodesia. And the change could not be a case of 'levelling up'; the economy of no African country could support a standard of living for all at the level now enjoyed by the White minorities in southern Africa.

Secondly, foreign trade and investment helps apartheid; it does not hinder it. Apartheid has become more repressive as South Africa has become richer. Indeed, continued White domination is only possible because increasing defence expenditure—of incredible proportions in African terms—can be financed out of a growing national income without calling for any real sacrifice from the white community. And that expenditure is not required against external enemies; it is needed to maintain the internal tyranny. 618 South African people were killed in the so-called 'riots' between June and December last year; two of them were Whites.

The truth is that foreign trade and investment are profitable. In 1970 the rate of return on direct U.S. investment in South Africa was 16.3 per cent; in other years it has been higher. The world rate was 11 per cent. All these investors were profiting from apartheid, and have an interest in sustaining it. For high South African profits, and low South African export prices, are possible only because of the apartheid racial wage-structure. Irritating as migrant labour, racial job-reservation, etc., may be to efficiency-minded businessmen, they can afford to accept them while they continue to pay to the Blacks wages which are too low to maintain a family.

United States' direct investment in South Africa has been increasing very fast in recent years. In 1966 its estimated total value was $490 million; by 1976 it was $1,600 million. The latter represents about 16 per cent of total American foreign investment. Current American investment in the rest of Africa has been estimated at $2,400 million.

American policies in relation to southern Africa are naturally determined by America, and in America's interests. But the U.S.A. is very powerful; it cannot avoid affecting developments in the rest of the world even if it wishes to do so. Africa therefore has a legitimate interest in American policies. Further, because the struggle for human dignity is one which both America and most African states have espoused, Africa feels it has the right to ask that American power should help, and not hinder its struggle for justice.

Africa is not asking for American military help. If U.S.A. was willing to provide weapons for the peoples' own struggles where war against the colonialists and racists has become inevitable, that would be welcome. But we do not want American Forces any more than we want Russian or Chinese Forces.

Africa is asking the U.S.A. to give political and economic support to the nationalist cause in southern Africa—and to the independent states like Zambia and Mozambique which are so badly hit by it. Indeed, on the basis of its own declared principles, it seems to us that America would be active in supporting the U.N. sanctions against Rhodesia; in backing up the U.N. attempts to get South Africa out of Namibia; and in furthering the isolation of the apartheid government of South Africa as a source of racialist infection for the whole world. In particular we would expect there to be special emphasis given to the arms embargo against South Africa and Rhodesia.

In the past these African expectations and hopes have not been fulfilled. In United Nations discussions about apartheid in South Africa, about freedom for Namibia, and about international opposition to the Smith Regime in Rhodesia, the U.S.A. and its allies have time and again supported South Africa. The American veto in the Security Council has been used to prevent international decisions adverse to these racialist minority governments. Further, not only have American firms and individuals evaded the U.N. sanctions against Rhodesia with impunity, even the U.S. Congress has authorized the purchase of Rhodesian chrome. American citizens have fought on the side of South Africa when it invaded Angola; American ex-servicemen are now fighting in the Smith army against the Freedom Fighters of Zimbabwe.

The first signs of a change in U.S.A. policies came in early 1976. Africa welcomed them, but soon came to the conclusion that they were half-hearted and prompted more by super-power competition than by a genuine concern for equality and justice in southern Africa. The main focus of your country's attention to these matters was still Russia, China and Cuba; not Africa.

During 1977 there have been American statements, and some actions, of a very different nature. The demand for Human Rights no longer appears to be just a stick with which to attack communist states; it seems to be a genuine effort to support justice in other states as well. The policy statements by President Carter and Secretary Vance; the clear line taken by Vice-President Mondale in his discussions with Mr. Vorster; the understanding revealed by the American Ambassador to the United Nations; all these things have given to Africa renewed hope, and the possibility of renewed faith in America.

This is not to say that there are no differences or disagreements between Tanzanian and American policies. Nor is it possible to wipe out in a few months the mutual suspicions which grew out of years of American practical support for the racialist states of southern Africa. And America is not a monolithic society, all of whose people automatically give full support to the actions of the government they elected.

But Africa neither produces miracles, nor expects them. What we see in current American policy is grounds for a belief that the U.S.A. is not automatically hostile to African aspirations for freedom, and an American recognition that African nationalism with its demand for racial equality, is a genuinely indigenous force—not an aspect of communist conspiracies against Western interests.

Possibilities of misunderstanding, and divergent American and African policies, remain. For slow and gradual change in southern Africa is no longer sufficient. Changes in southern African governments or social structures which might some ten or fifteen years ago have been welcomed as a sign of hope, are now irrelevant. Too many people have died in the meantime; too many false hopes have been aroused and betrayed.

In Rhodesia, time has completely run out. The only way the war can be stopped is by a transfer of power to the majority. If combined British and American action can quickly achieve such a transfer of power—in real terms, which includes ending the power of the present Smith army—only the people of Zimbabwe themselves could be happier than I would be. We in Tanzania support the attempt; we do not have much hope of its success, for we know Ian Smith and his colleagues.

In Namibia also, Tanzania welcomes the attempt now being made by America and its allies to secure a South African evacuation of the territory, and the establishment of a government based on the principles of unity and non-racialism. Again, we do not have much hope of its success; we understand—and to some extent share—the suspicions of SWAPO. But it does seem to us now that this attempt is genuine, and motivated by a desire to secure a peaceful but real transfer of power to the people of Namibia.

There could be a little time for peaceful change in South Africa; the war between the non-whites, and the White government under which they suffer, has not yet started. With all its dangers of becoming a straightforward race war, with terrible implications for the world, it could still be avoided if the need for fundamental change was accepted, and the process begun. But there is no sign that this last-minute opportunity will be seized by the white minority. For cosmetic changes in apartheid are only insulting; it is not permission to stay in an expensive hotel which is the issue, it is the right to live in decency and dignity. If the South African Whites really want to avoid disaster for themselves and their country, they will talk to the Africans of South Africa. This means discussions with genuine African nationalist leaders like Mandela, Sisulu, Sobukwe*—and also with the young people who have stepped forward since these older campaigners for freedom were imprisoned. American pressure on South Africa to move in this direction is very welcome; it will need to be greatly intensified before it achieves progress.

Mr. Chairman: I have no 'solution' for the problems of southern Africa. I know that America cannot provide one. Any solution will have to be worked out between all the peoples of southern Africa—all those who have made their homes in that part of my continent regardless of their colour, race, or religion. But of one thing I am quite sure. Peace, and progress towards human rights for all, can only come when there is national independence on the basis of majority rule in each country, and on the basis of human equality. For although racial prejudice cannot be eliminated by constitutional change, it is only when racial equality is enshrined in the legal structure of the state, and when the government is committed to building it, that peace and co-operation between men becomes a possibility.

It is our hope that America will use its great influence, and a little of its power, to support those who struggle against great odds for justice—and therefore for ultimate peace—in southern Africa.

---

* Mangaliso Robert Sobukwe died on 26 February 1978 of lung cancer at Kimberley Hospital, where he had been admitted after a long detention on Robben Island.

SEVEN

Sunday, 7 August, is spent witnessing agricultural activities at the University of California, Davis Campus. Then Nyerere flies out to Los Angeles. It is here that he tells the United States that he welcomes the continued stay of Cuban troops in Angola and warns that more will be asked for unless the United States tells South Africa to desist from acts of provocation against the Peoples' Republic of Angola.

Before proceeding to his first mayoral dinner in the U.S. hosted by Mayor and Mrs. Tom Bradley, Nyerere is treated to a plush reception hosted by two Afro-American show-business celebrities, Clarence Avant and Sidney Poitier and their wives. This is in appreciation of his contribution to the liberation struggle throughout Africa.

At the dinner, Nyerere replies to Mayor Bradley:

Mr. Mayor, Mrs. Bradley, and Friends,
First let me say how much I appreciate the warm welcome which has been given to me in Los Angeles—and indeed in California generally. And you have been very kind in your remarks, Mr. Mayor; I can assure you that I feel at least equal pleasure in returning to Los Angeles, and particularly in meeting you and your colleagues in the city.

Mr. Mayor; as I have indicated, this is not my first visit to Los Angeles. But last time I was in your city for even less time than on this occasion, making little more than a night stop before returning to Washington to meet the then campaigner for presidential office, President Kennedy. And in 1960 you were a senior officer in the City Police, while I was Leader of the Opposition in what was still the Trusteeship Territory of Tanganyika; I confess I do not recall that we met! Both of us have heavier responsibilities now!

We in Tanzania read about American politics, and American elections—sometimes including mayoral elections! And your two campaigns for the position you now hold were well publicized, Mr. Mayor—they appear to have been the kind of tough political battles which make good newspaper copy! But you seem to have survived very well—and to be flourishing in the face of the daunting tasks which face the government of a city like this one, with its three million inhabitants, its rapid growth and heavy pollution problems. So I will, even at this late date, offer to you my congratulations on your election, and my very best wishes for the success of the efforts which you, your colleagues, and the people of your city are making to improve the conditions of people's lives, and the environment in which you all live.

May I therefore ask that everyone joins me in a Toast:
To Mayor Bradley,
to Mrs Bradley,
and the welfare of
all the people of
Los Angeles.

EIGHT

At the conclusion of his two-day stay in America's West, Nyerere flies to the South touching down first at Tullahoma, the headquarters of the Tennessee Valley Authority, the irrigation, hydroelectric, fishing, waterway and flood control complex. Nyerere's interest in this project lies in its similarity with the Rufiji Basin Development Authority, currently under development back home in Tanzania.

But Nyerere is not in the U.S. to seek assistance for Tanzania. Indeed at the end of their White House talks Nyerere answered *no* when Carter specifically asked if there were any bilateral questions he wished to raise. Not that Tanzania would not welcome U.S. assistance to augment her own efforts in solving her multiple development problems. But the liberation of southern Africa is the priority on this trip. So that even though the day is spent visiting economic projects Nyerere grabs the first opportunity at Governor Ray Blanton's dinner in Nashville that evening to return to the subject of the crusade—liberation.

The basic theme in this and other speeches he makes thereafter, is a challenge to the American people to rally behind their President in combining the American ethic of liberty and the American power behind the struggling peoples of southern Africa.

Mr. Governor and Friends,
I have been speaking a lot since I arrived in your country some five days ago, and now I am nearing the end of the visit, I would like to use this opportunity to do two things: one; to thank you very much on my own behalf and on behalf of my colleagues for your reception and for the kind things you have been saying about myself, about my country and the understanding that you have shown to our problems.

The second thing I am going to say, I have to say with an apology; I have visited your country several times. Before my country became independent, I used to come to the United Nations as a petitioner. My country was a trust territory under the United Nations. And we discovered that we could pressurize the British through world public opinion. So I used to come to the United Nations to build up a little amount of pressure against the British. I know the British a little bit. I know they can be pressurized. And so several times I came to the United Nations and eventually I knew that as far as building world public opinion against British occupation of Tanzania was concerned, I had done the necessary job. I stopped coming to the United Nations and decided to concentrate on organizing the people in Tanzania.

But I didn't stop coming to your country. When the State Department realized that we were winning—the British were on the way out—they thought I was worth inviting. So they invited me in a programme which they called a 'leadership grant' or something like that. I came and I stayed for some time in Washington and they arranged for me to go to California which I did. I didn't spend very much time in California. I spent a few hours, I think twenty-four hours or so, and then I got a message that the then Senator Kennedy would like a meeting. I thought it was very important. I had met Senator Kennedy in 1957 on one of my petition visits. I had noticed at that time that he already had ambitions of going a bit higher. So when he asked me to go and meet him in 1960, I hurried back to Washington and met him.

My country became independent in 1961. Early in 1963 I wrote to President Kennedy about our problems in southern Africa. I wrote to him because we had both been under the British Empire, your country and mine.

I was a teacher. I taught the history of the British Empire, which means I taught a bit of the history of your country. I wrote to him because I knew the manner and the promise with which your country came into being.

But that was not the only reason. For one thing your country gave that independence manifesto to the world: 'all men are created equal'. For the other, I knew also that your country had power. I felt that a combination of your national ethic and that power could be of use to people all over the world who want liberation. He wrote back saying 'Look, we can't discuss such serious matters through writing. Why don't you come to Washington for talks?'

So I came to Washington to discuss southern Africa. That was fourteen years ago. I didn't come back until President Carter was elected and I am here for the same purpose. So I want to apologize to you that every time I come here, I come to talk 'shop'. I hope one day it is going to be possible for me to come to your country not to talk 'shop'.

But at present there is serious business. Our continent is not free. The idea of colonialism is now anachronistic in the rest of the world. It's absurd that in 1977 we should have colonies anywhere on this planet, but we have colonies. It is absurd that two hundred years after your people said all men are created equal, we should have a state in the world which has a racial philosophy, whose laws and whose practices of government are based on racial discrimination, in 1977, not 1777!

You have that ethic and you have the power. And you have a President in Washington who, I think, can be usefully reminded of that ethic and that power. I am asking you to help us. I do not know what you are going to remember your President for. But just now, I think, he is going to be remembered, certainly in the rest of the world, for his emphasis on human rights. If the problem of human rights in your country is no longer an issue, I don't think you will remember him for it. But for us it is a serious issue. And so, outside of your own country, we are beginning to identify your President with the struggle for human rights.

I have a feeling that because of your ethic and because of Vietnam, you are proud of your President. You feel he has the ability to build a different kind of image for your country in the rest of the world. I am asking you to help him, to help us. And I am saying specifically, you cannot help your President if you continue to ignore the problems of southern Africa. You are the citizens of the most powerful country in the world; a country which started a revolution, a real, articulated revolution, about human rights. You started it and the French followed. I am saying as citizens of the country you cannot help your President very much, if you continue ignoring the problems of southern Africa.

But worse still, you can't help your President, if you continue investing money in South Africa, backing up the government of that country, giving it power, giving it strength. Don't pay for racialism in southern Africa. You don't need South Africa. It's a small country. It's powerful in African terms but its an immoral country. Don't pay South Africa. You don't need them, Governor; they need you. But they embarrass you. Your ethic requires you to isolate them. Your power requires you to support the victims of that philosophy.

You have a Governor; you have a President who understands this, so I am asking you to back him up because going from capital to capital in the Western World, I have discovered that democracy is being used as an alibi for not doing the right thing in southern Africa. You sit down with a head of government, with a head of state; you explain these problems of racialism in southern Africa; you say don't do this, or do this in order to help us. He says, 'Yes, Mr. President, I understand you, but I lead a democratic society; they will not understand.' Democracy is used as an excuse for continuing to support evil. And I am asking you Governor and all my friends in your country, please, we have a serious problem in southern Africa, it's a problem of human rights. Those racists in southern Africa need your help. So far you have given them that help; stop giving them that help.

Having said that, Governor, I want to say once more, I thank you very much for the welcome that you have given to me and my colleagues, and for the understanding that the people of your country have shown us everywhere since we arrived in this country. Thank you very much.

NINE

In the morning of 9 August, Nyerere arrives at Tifton, Georgia, the last state he is to visit. Morning and afternoon are spent observing more agricultural development projects,

including a heavily mechanized scheme for groundnut and maize farming.

At the Tifton luncheon hosted by the Tifton Chamber of Commerce, main speaker Professor D.W. Brooks emphasizes increased production as the only way for the poor countries of the world to raise the living standards of their peoples. He pointedly notes that no matter how good the policies a country pursues, development would stagnate without emphasis on increased productivity. That in his view ought to be the priority for the poor countries of the world.

Professor Brooks, perhaps inadvertently, opens the way for Nyerere's argument that no matter how hard the poor of the world work, they will not develop until and unless the present world economic order is abandoned.

Friends, my function is to say a sincere thank you very much to you. I've now been in your country for a few days and tomorrow I am leaving.

It is not easy in such a short time to learn a great deal about a large country like yours, but that short time I've been here is enough to make me and my colleagues to leave your country with immense hope.

Yours is a very powerful country. Sometimes we fear it. I first visited the U.S.A. officially in 1963, at the invitation of President Kennedy. I came to discuss southern Africa and I left greatly encouraged.

I am back this time on a state visit. But it is a different kind of state visit from the state visits I have been paying in other countries. It is a business state visit—I am still here to seek the assistance of your government and the American people, on our problems in southern Africa.

We have problems of liberation and I 've been talking about them. But we don't want liberation for the sake of liberation. We don't simply want to get to govern our countries merely for the sake of putting up a flag and having a national anthem and having a seat at the United Nations. It does happen that my country is the United Republic of Tanzania and yours is the United States of America. At the United Nations we sit very close because the seats are arranged in alphabetical order. Theoretically we are equal. But you know we are not.

So I say, we have been talking about our problems of liberation in southern Africa. But we have other problems: the problems of development, which you have been talking about. Professor, I do agree with everything that you have said. We have to increase our productivity. We have to use modern science, we have to get it to our own people, we have to encourage our people through incentives.

If people are going to work, they must work knowing that they are going to reap the benefits of their work. They should not work like a bunch of slaves. They should work for themselves and know that they are working for their own good.

So Professor, I agree with everything you say and that is why I am here. I'm here to learn how and what you do in raising peanuts. We grow peanuts. We call them groundnuts. We love them. Some of us eat them raw. We eat peanuts as you eat candy. But productivity is not very good. It is very poor as you know. So we have these problems of increasing the productivity of the farmer. These are problems that we have and we know them. In too many of our poor countries, the poor countries of the Third World, the people work and some have succeeded in raising productivity, but the benefits go to a small ruling élite. The benefits don't go to the masses of the people. That's an internal problem. The problem of raising productivity in Tanzania is mine. The problem of seeing that what is produced goes to the masses of the people is mine.

But there is another problem. I believe it is the biggest problem now facing the poor countries. This is the problem of the system of the world.

I don't make my own tractors in Tanzania. I've got to buy tractors from here. I must increase my productivity. But I find that the price of your tractors is going up and up and up, and I am not very sure with the price of my sisal or my cotton. Because of this I have to sell more and more tons of sisal every year to buy the same type of tractor.

If the productivity per acre is good, fine, I can produce more cotton per acre, more cotton per hectare. But more and more in order to buy the same tractor. This I can't do anything about. This is the world's system, about which I cannot do anything. This has to be tackled internationally. And that's where the industrialized countries must help us.

We are going to work hard, to increase our knowledge and to

increase our productivity. We are going to work hard in some of our own countries to change the exploitative system in those countries so that if our people work, they reap the benefits of their work. But the international system I can do very little about. That is one.

I gave the example of the tractor. It's better for me to export textiles rather than raw cotton. I will improve the value of this product if I can process it before I sell it. But the industrialized countries will not let us sell our textiles to them. They will have tariff barriers and if they don't have tariff barriers, they will have quota barriers. Why? They say, because wages are lower in our countries than they are in their countries. This is 'sweated labour'. But the wages in the textile factory in Tanzania are higher than the price which I give to the peasant who produces cotton! But the cotton I can sell to Europe, no problem. But if I tried to sell textile to them, they say, no, no, no, this is sweated labour! They are protecting the industrialized countries. They are protecting their markets. These are the biggest markets. They would rather buy my cotton, they would rather buy my fibre, but the moment I begin to sell textiles, the moment I try to sell rope or twine, I am in trouble. That includes the U.S. I find it more difficult to sell twine here.

So, Professor, there are problems which are Tanzania problems and I am going to handle them. I am going to try and handle those internal problems; and with the help of friends like you here I'll bring students here. My Minister for Agriculture says he brought only eighteen this year—eighteen agricultural students. I'll bring large numbers of students, if you can allow me. I'll bring large numbers of students to come and learn. They will take your knowledge back and will increase our productivity. But even when we have solved the internal problem of productivity, of justice within Tanzania, the problem of justice internationally will remain, and there you can help us. Friends, once again I thank you very much for your hospitality and for your understanding of our problems. Thank you very much.

TEN

Atlanta has been honoured to be the last state capital Nyerere will visit before he leaves for home. And it lives up to the honour. Governor George Busby and Mayor Maynard Jackson lead the city into a moving welcome for Nyerere

that afternoon and a lavish dinner that night. Nyerere's theme at the dinner remains the same—a challenge to the American people's conscience not to sustain apartheid and racial domination through political and economic support for the systems obtaining in southern Africa.

Governor Busby, Mayor Jackson, Distinguished Guests, Ladies and Gentlemen,
This is my last evening in your country, and I would like to take this opportunity to thank you very much on my own behalf and on behalf of my colleagues for the great kindness that the people of your country and your state and city have shown to us since our arrival.

I visited your country many times as a petitioner. For before my country became independent, it was a United Nations' trust territory under the administration of the United Kingdom. I used to come to the United Nations to petition for the independence of my country. But by profession I am a teacher. I taught the history of the British Empire. You may have forgotten that you were under the British Empire. So I have taught your history. In that history I was told that the British had learned after your war of independence, not to insist on governing a people that want to become self-governing. But the British learned to grant independence to White colonies. South Africa was the exception that proves the rule, because whites there included Boers. But South Africa became independent.

After that, the British forgot the lesson they had learned from you. We had to start all over again and it was not until after the Second World War that I am told your then President, Franklin Delano Roosevelt, had a discussion with the British Prime Minister, Winston Churchill, in which he asked him, 'Aren't we fighting for democracy and freedom and India wants independence?'

Churchill, I am told, answered him by saying, 'I did not become His Majesty's first Minister, in order to preside over the dissolution of the Empire.' But after that India became independent. Today Africa is virtually free. But if George Washington came back today, two hundred years since you became independent of the British rule, and heard me speak about freedom, he would say, 'You are still struggling? Two hundred years, and Rhodesia is still a British colony?'

In the South of the United States, you have a history of slavery. But even when you still had slavery, your Founding Fathers said, 'All men are equal'. And now you still have racial prejudice in this country. I still have very silly people in my country who have racial prejudice. Racialism is one of the most irrational things in the world. But racial prejudice held by individuals, is different from a racial philosophy upheld through state legislation.

We have only one country in the whole world, where the philosophy of racial prejudice is the basis of government legislation. That country is South Africa.

My first state visit here in 1963, at the invitation of President John F. Kennedy, was to discuss South Africa. This is my second state visit. A great honour to me by President Carter. As in 1963, I have come here because I feel there is a President who understands what we are talking about. So here I am again as a petitioner.

I am sure you can understand why it is not possible for us in Africa to continue to live in colonialism or racialism. We have to destroy colonialism and racialism. I am here to plead that you combine your own ethic that all men are created equal and your power to help us to end racialism and colonialism in Africa.

I am going back feeling that that message has been understood, and I am thanking you very much for that understanding.

ELEVEN

It is 10 August, the last morning of Nyerere's stay in the U.S. Breakfast has been laid on and Atlanta civic leaders have been invited. Nyerere again calls on them to support their President in his moves to back up human rights in southern Africa. And in the final news conference before Mwalimu leaves the U.S., he once more speaks on the need for the American people to back up the oppressed in southern Africa.

PRESS: How do the people of Tanzania view racialism in the United States?

PRESIDENT: We know that you have a history of racial tension.

We know that at one time you had a system of slavery here. We know that you have not completely solved your racial problems; we haven't solved our racial problems either. We come from an inherited system, where race was used as the base of social organization. For instance, at independence in Tanzania, we had European, Asian and African schools. We had to abolish these racial segregations in education and health, after independence. We still have some racial prejudice, but the legislation of the country is non-racial and we know that the legislation of your own country is non-racial. So we make a distinction between racial tensions in areas like southern Africa, where the laws of the country are based on race, and the racial tensions of a country like yours, where the laws of the country are no longer based on race. You still have to fight racial prejudice.

PRESS: Will President Carter's appointment of Andrew Young to the United Nations really help the general relationship between the United States and the Front Line States of Botswana, Angola, Mozambique, Zambia and Tanzania?

PRESIDENT: Not necessarily. The mere appointment of a black American would not have made the slightest difference. What could make a difference and I believe will make a difference, is the fact that the Carter administration appears to be determined to throw its weight behind the movement for liberation and the ending of racialism in southern Africa and no longer regards those who struggle against racialism and colonialism in Africa as being agents of communism. It is that which makes the difference, not the appointment of Young, except that, the appointment of Young is an indication of a change in policy.

PRESS: You said at Howard University that charity in the form of aid is not what is needed for the harmonious development of the world. What would you like to see?

PRESIDENT: We want a changed system. I'll try to explain. You can't end poverty through charity. You have not tried to end poverty in your own country, here, through charity. Within a single nation, you don't end poverty through charity. You get people to work, you allow them to work, you get jobs for them, you get them trained and they work.

And when they work, you want to make sure that they earn the return for their work. You tax people. In your own country, here, some people are richer than others. Even in this country, where I think the gap between the rich and the poor is very large, you still tax the rich more in order that you can get money. I am explaining what is done. It may not be done to the extent that is desirable. But I'm saying the theory is accepted, that the rich are taxed in order that you may try to reduce the gap between the poor and the rich. They are taxed. They are not asked to pay voluntarily.

I'm told that the Southern States, for instance, used to grow cotton and their cotton used to go to the North, and it is the North which would make the textiles. Then, the textiles would come back to the South. The South never liked that. They wanted to be in a position to grow the cotton, to process their own cotton, to make the textiles and then sell the textiles.

Now, we the Third World countries are in that position with the rest of the world. Of course, we have to work in Tanzania. Of course, we have to raise our skills. Of course, we have to raise our productivity on the land and per person. But then, when I try to use that money in order to buy a tractor, I find that I have to use more and more tons of sisal or coffee, or cotton, in order to buy the same kind of tractor. So that my increased productivity simply keeps me at the same level as I was. I'll try to sell finished products naturally, as the Southern States in the United States discovered very early. It is no use selling raw materials. It is better to process. So, I try to process.

But finding the markets for my finished products is very difficult. I find it very difficult to sell textiles to the developed countries. They call it a free market and they protect it with tariff barriers with quota systems and so forth.

We want two things. We want a system of trade which does not have a built-in mechanism, which transfers wealth from the poor to the rich. This is what happens now. At present, there is a built-in mechanism which transfers wealth from the poor to the rich. We want this changed. I want to be able, if I work harder, to buy two tractors next year instead of one. At present, this does not happen. We want to be able to have a say in the financial institutions of the world. At present, we have very little say in the World Bank or in the I.M.F. These are dominated by the rich countries. We borrow money in order to finance our development projects. We find that every year we have to borrow money in order to pay the debts. Now, this is not good. You can't develop like this, and so we want a system which, in fact, would be the equivalent of taxing the rich in order to try and reduce het gap between the rich and the poor. We want the equivalent of a fair wage so that if the Third World countries work hard, they should be able to reap the benefits of their efforts.

PRESS: Mr. President, Sir, you're quoted as saying that if the U.S. get involved in the guerrilla fighting in southern Africa the war could be over soon. Would you explain to us a little bit more on how the United States could be involved?

PRESIDENT: No, No, No. I don't want to embarrass my host. We are involved in the guerrilla fighting. We are asking nobody to get involved in the guerrilla fighting. We get arms, but we don't get arms from the United States or from any of the Western countries. We do get arms from the communist countries. If the United States offers me arms, I will take them and give them to the guerrilla fighters. But I am not likely to get them and that is why I'm not asking for arms. But in the past, whenever we have tried to get pressures applied internationally, by the international community at the United Nations, your country and her allies have used their 'veto' to keep South Africa amongst the respected community in the world. You have thrown your power behind racialism in southern Africa, and until recently, you were abrogating the sanctions of the United Nations against Rhodesia. It is of immense assistance to racialism in southern Africa. In the past, you have done this, and because you did that, you strengthened the minorities, the oppressors. If you change and you begin to throw your diplomatic weight, your economic weight (not your military weight) behind the liberation movements, I say that can shorten the war. That's what I'm saying. I'm not suggesting that you should join the guerrilla fighters.

PRESS: How good is your liaison with the Russians?

PRESIDENT: The liaison is very good. If by liaison you mean, have I enough contact with them so that when I don't have enough arms I can say, 'Eh!, increase the supply'. If that is what you mean, 'Yes'. I have a Russian Ambassador, I have a United States Ambassador, and so I keep contact with them. I need the support of the Russians, I need the support of the United States. I have Ambassadors, both in Moscow and in Washington, and both Moscow and Washington have Ambassadors in Dar es Salaam. So, we are very close and from each super power, I try to get what it can give, what its politics allow it to give, to help us in the liberation movement. The Russians can give us arms, you cannot give us arms, but there are other things you can give us and that's what I'm here for.

PRESS: Does this not indebt you to the Russians?

PRESIDENT: Owe them what?

PRESS: A little allegiance perhaps?

PRESIDENT: What allegiance? There is no doubt that, if I am in trouble and I seek help which you have and which you deny me, or worse still, you give the help to my enemy—the other one gives me that aid; naturally, I would be more friendly to the one who gives me aid. It is a natural thing, isn't it? If the United States really throws its power behind the racists in southern Africa, but the communist countries help us, naturally, we appreciate the aid from the communist countries! When you give aid to the racists of southern Africa you will be appreciated by the racists, not by us.

PRESS: What about receiving Cuban troops?

PRESIDENT: I find an incredible obsession with Cuba. Frankly, I really don't understand this at all. Cuba is a tiny little island country, ninety miles off the coast of the United States. I think nine million people, and yet, there is a tremendous amount of obsession with Cuba, including, I think, some indications that United States relations with Cuba will not be normalized until the Cubans have removed their troops from Angola. This I don't understand. We need arms. We don't make arms in Africa. Little Cuba has some arms. We go round to see where we can get arms and little Cuba can give us arms—at a great cost to themselves, because they need these arms themselves. They get some of these arms from the Soviet Union and they pay for them. I don't believe they get them free. They supply those arms. It is the arms we take and I think Joshua Nkomo made it very clear. It is the arms he needs, not men. He has the men. He doesn't want the Cubans to fight for him. Incidentally, the Angolans won their war against the Portuguese without the slightest assistance from a single person from Cuba. They won their independence on their own. The Cubans were needed to fight against the invading South Africans, and also the Americans. You were backing up a bunch of reactionaries in Angola, and you really were trying to throw your weight behind people who had not fought during the war against the Portuguese at all because you feared that the Peoples' Movement for the Liberation of Angola was communist. They had to seek assistance and they got assistance from Cuba—both people and material. But that was the first time they did it, because, the threat was from your people and from the South Africans.

PRESS: Can you go into a little more detail as to what kind of assistance President Carter has promised?

PRESIDENT: I can't. I can't go into a little more detail. I can say I would like your country to STOP supporting racialism—that is very clear. I would like your country to see if they can help the liberation movements. You will have to decide what kind of help you can give us.

PRESS: Have you been impressed that President Carter is serious about the liberation of southern Africa?

PRESIDENT: I have. I would be less than frank if I say I was not impressed by President Carter's seriousness about ending racialism and colonialism in southern Africa. I have a feeling that he will try. But frankly, it is not a question of the Administration. All governments have to move their systems and it does not matter how committed a president is, he has got to move a system. I don't know how easy it is to move your system. But I repeat, your President has impressed me very much and very many people in the world that he is serious about human rights all over the world. And that, whenever possible, he is going to try within limits to put his weight behind those forces which are fighting for human rights. But he has got to be assisted by people in this country.

Now you have powerful people here. You have powerful multinational companies, which invest a lot of money in southern Africa. Yet, the same people would like their President to work for human rights; and these same people would undermine him because they invest in racialism, in apartheid in southern Africa, and they reap the benefits of racialism and apartheid. You will have to act too!

PRESS: Do you believe Andrew Young is a believer or just a symbol of what Carter wants done?

PRESIDENT: I believe Andrew Young is not a symbol, he is a believer. He believes in what he says. I don't think he makes a show. I think the reactionaries don't like him because they know that he is a believer, that what he says he believes. I'm told there is an attempt to turn him into a different type of person. But, we believe that for President Carter to appoint not just a black man, but a black who believes in human rights, is more than a symbol.

PRESS: So what are you going to say to Secretary Vance about your talks in Washington?

PRESIDENT: Actually, it's what Secretary Vance is going to say to me rather than what I'm going to say to him. During my discussions with President Carter, he said that Secretary Vance would be meeting with David Owen and I think possibly Pik Botha, the South African Foreign Minister, and he thought that if I was passing through London, it might be a good thing for Secretary Vance to brief me on their London discussions.

PRESS: Mr. President, is there any future in pan-Africanism and can Africa do anything about tensions between two African countries?

PRESIDENT: There is a future in pan-African unity. Naturally, we are going to go through ups and downs in building unity over our continent, but even those of us who sometimes feel a little frustrated, a little uneasy about the movement toward unity in Africa, still realize that ours, the O.A.U., is a unique organization. There is no other in the world. It is a continental organization. No other continent has the kind of organization that we have, the O.A.U.

So, we have something there and we hope it will learn and it will strengthen itself. Now, can we do something about these tensions which take place between two African countries? We do try. We have no military power. We can't send a military force and separate two countries which are at each other's throat, but as I'm speaking now, there is a concialiation committee of the Organization of African Unity meeting now in Libreville in order to see whether they can lower the tension between Ethiopia and Somalia. But we can only persuade. There is nothing more we can do.

PRESS: Do you know if the U.S. is putting pressure on South Africa not to explode a nuclear bomb?

PRESIDENT: I don't know. The South Africans, I am sure, are making nuclear weapons to frighten us. I know that President Carter and the other nuclear powers would like to limit the spread of nuclear weapons. So, I suppose they will disapprove of South

Africa's intention to build nuclear weapons. I don't think they can succeed if the South Africans are determined. I think they will make nuclear weapons. But the South Africans have to be told that, however many nuclear bombs they make, we are not going to be deterred. We will go on fighting, and we will win.

Your country has a lot of nuclear weapons, and you went in to Vietnam. You pulled out of Vietnam. The South Africans are preparing for the wrong war. If they want to drop a nuclear bomb on Dar es Salaam, they can. Let them go ahead and drop a nuclear bomb on Dar es Salaam. But to defeat opposition to apartheid they will have to drop nuclear bombs in Johannesburg and Cape Town and Durban, and that they will not do.

They can go ahead, with the bomb. But, we will defeat them. I have said that South Africa is an African state with a large white minority. We are going to fight until we get one-man-one vote in South Africa. We will get democracy in South Africa. South Africa is going to be the first black African state with nuclear weapons. I am serious.

TWELVE

Jamaica has been and continues to be one of the most consistent backers of the African liberation struggle. With this in view President Nyerere flies over to the island at the end of his U.S. state visit, basically to brief Prime Minister Michael Manley, his government, his party and his people on the state of the struggle.

Nyerere thus spends three days in Montego Bay, before proceeding to London.

Meanwhile, President Carter in a follow-up to the talks he has had with Nyerere, has asked his Secretary of State Cyrus Vance to meet Nyerere in London where he would be enroute to Dar es Salaam. Vance is to brief Nyerere on the talks he has had in London with the South African Foreign Minister, Pik Botha.

Something curious and as yet unexplained happens meantime. Having heard of Nyerere's transit stop of several hours in London and the arranged meeting with Vance, British Prime Minister James Callaghan also asks to see Nyerere. But he wants the latter to call on him at his Chequers country home for a luncheon meeting. Nyerere has sent word that he already has meetings scheduled with Vance and other leaders at the airport. That would make it difficult for him to drive all the way out to Chequers and still keep those other appointments. Would Callaghan come to the airport instead?

That triggers it. 'Nyerere snubs Callaghan', and 'Rhodesia talks in jeopardy as Nyerere refuses to meet Callaghan', run headlines in several of London's morning and evening newspapers. And for three days in a row, British newspapers, radio and television vie to outdo one another in portraying Nyerere the stubborn.

And no amount of explaining through the diplomatic channels seems to suffice. The impression is persistently being created that Nyerere's failure to attend that luncheon is a snub to Callaghan. A relatively junior British diplomat in Kingston phones one of Nyerere's aides to say Premier Callaghan would be 'annoyed' if Nyerere failed to accept the luncheon invitation. He goes as far as to say this would 'sour' the relations between Tanzania and the United Kingdom.

So when Julius Nyerere lands at London's Heathrow airport that morning, he finds a well orchestrated campaign to show him as a man who has snubbed the British Prime Minister.

At the end of his half hour meeting with Secretary Vance, Nyerere addresses the British Press which so persistently dwells on the 'snub' as if this, rather than the removal of the illegal racist rule of Ian Smith in Rhodesia, is the issue!

PRESS: Mr. President, are you going to accept the Anglo-American proposals for Rhodesia?

PRESIDENT: I will have to wait until I know what the Anglo-American proposals for Rhodesia are; and if those proposals do solve our problems, why should I not accept them?

PRESS: Well, and the new Constitution and safeguard for law and order and the £700 million development fund?

PRESIDENT: I am not going to form the government of independent Zimbabwe, so the multi-million dollar development fund is for the future government of Zimbabwe to talk about. My function is to get Smith out of the way and his power structure. And if the Anglo-American proposals are helping us to achieve that objective—getting Smith out and his power structure and getting an elected government coming in on the basis of one-man-one-vote—then of course, I will back them up.

PRESS: Are you going to lunch with the British Prime Minister?

PRESIDENT: No.

PRESS: Are you going to see him?

PRESIDENT: I am not aware that I am seeing him.

PRESS: It is being seen, Mr. President, as a snub that you are not attending the Chequers' lunch. Were you intending to snub the British?

PRESIDENT: Who is talking about this snub?

PRESS: It is in general speculation that it has been a snub.

PRESIDENT: Who is talking about this blessed snub? I am passing through London on my way back to Dar es Salaam, and here I am.

PRESS: But you were in fact to lunch with the Prime Minister; why did you refuse?

PRESIDENT: What do you mean? I can have lunch with the Prime Minister at any time, really; I did not refuse to have lunch with the Prime Minister. I don't know who is saying this. I have not refused to lunch with the Prime Minister—I have not refused having lunch and talking with the Prime Minister. I don't know who is saying this.

PRESS: You are perfectly prepared . . .

PRESIDENT: Please, I am perfectly prepared to have lunch with the Prime Minister, to have talks with the Prime Minister any time.

PRESS: Are you saying, perhaps, you have not been invited to have lunch and talks with the Prime Minister?

PRESIDENT: Look, I know you people are very carefully briefed and you know what is happening. But look, I am ready to have talks with the Prime Minister. Do you realize that I have just had talks here with the American Secretary of State Mr. Cyrus Vance? Why should I say I don't want to have talks with the Prime Minister of Britain. I am in Britain. Who is suggesting that

I am refusing to talk to the Prime Minister of Britain when I am here in Britain? I have just had talks with the Secretary of State, Vance, and then I would say that I do not want to have talks with the Prime Minister of Britain, why? Where would I get this idea? I don't know who is putting out these ideas at all.

PRESS: Mr. President, Mr. Vance said earlier that he has been encouraged by your talks this morning. Can you tell us what you told him that gave him this encouragement?

PRESIDENT: We were both encouraged. I am glad Mr. Vance said that he was encouraged. I was encouraged by my whole visit in the United States. During talks with President Carter, I have explained what it is we are trying to achieve in Zimbabwe and I find there is understanding of what we are trying to do and the willingness to help us to achieve our objective.

PRESS: What was the outcome of your talks this morning with Mr. Vance. I mean, what did you tell Mr. Vance that encouraged him from the talks?

PRESIDENT: Shouldn't you ask Mr. Vance that?

PRESS: Mr. President, do you think a peaceful solution is possible in Rhodesia?

PRESIDENT: No, it is not possible. We are fighting. What we are talking about is how to end that war. A peaceful solution was ruled out by Smith ages ago. They are now fighting. As I am talking now, people are dying there. So what is possible is to end that war. We are discussing with the Americans whether we can end that war. What we are talking about is how to end that war.

PRESS: You have the details of the initiative. What will you be saying to the other African Presidents? I mean, what will you be recommending to them?

PRESIDENT: I will not recommend anything to my colleagues when I meet them. I will recommend nothing at all. I will tell them I have been trying to find out whether President Carter is willing to put some of his power behind the liberation movement.

PRESS: Mr. President, did you decide anything with Mr. Vance this morning?

PRESIDENT: We found that we are talking the same language. It is very encouraging to find out that the Secretary of State of the United States can be talking the same language with somebody who is trying to achieve independence for Zimbabwe.

PRESS: Mr. President, can you give us indications?

PRESIDENT: No, I really cannot.

PRESS: The talks were very useful this morning.

PRESIDENT: Very useful.

PRESS: I want to ask you, Mr. President, what you thought about the South African presence here on those talks. Does it appear to you the talks are in fact tripartite?

PRESIDENT: Both the British and the Americans have always regarded the South Africans to be a key element in any solution in southern Africa. I think they are. But I have always said it is wrong to try and use the South Africans as allies in achieving majority rule in Rhodesia. These fellows cannot be our allies. These fellows are the pillar of racialism in southern Africa. Precisely because they are the supporters of Smith, what you really need is to say, 'Look here, we want to achieve majority rule in Rhodesia and don't stand in the way.' But whichever way you look at them they are important.

PRESS: Mr. President, do you, therefore, see them standing in the way?

PRESIDENT: They have been standing in the way. There were two countries, only two countries in the whole world which were officially breaking the sanctions against Rhodesia and they were Portugal and South Africa. They were doing that. The South Africans are still breaking the sanctions against Rhodesia. They are still the major prop of the Smith regime.

PRESS: Was this brought up this morning with Mr. Vance?

PRESIDENT: No, I was not discussing this. I am not discussing South Africa.

PRESS: Dr. Owen said that he would be visiting South Africa possibly this year or next year. Do you think he can achieve anything?

PRESIDENT: I do not know. All I am convinced of now is that at least Americans do not regard guerrilla fighting as the introduction of communism in southern Africa. They take it for what it is. It is a struggle for liberation the same way as they fought for their own liberation. Now that this is the American attitude, given that understanding, and given their support, there is no reason why their support, your support and our pressures should not bring about the required result.

PRESS: But do you think the trip by Mr. Owen could achieve anything more?

PRESIDENT: I do not know what importance you are putting to a trip. If they have agreed and Owen thinks it is important to explain to some people about what they have agreed, a trip as such cannot do anything. It is really the package, it is what that trip is about. And if the trip is about explaining something which is concrete, of course it would achieve something.

PRESS: Mr. President, I want to take you back to the question you were asked earlier on about your non-meeting with the Prime Minister while you are here. Are you saying in fact, as you said before, that you would see the Prime Minister if he had come to greet you or meet you at the airport?

PRESIDENT: I do not know why this thing is a big issue. You will have to explain to me why being in transit and being unable to go to Chequers because I am in transit is a big diplomatic issue. Why is it? I am in transit going back to Dar es Salaam. I have just been talking to Vance here.

PRESS: A Head of State arriving in this country expressing a wish to see the Prime Minister; the Prime Minister says, 'Yes, by all means see me', but the meeting does not come off . . . .

PRESIDENT: Who told you this?

PRESS: We understand . . .

PRESIDENT: It is a lie!

PRESIDENT: I don't want to get involved in this because some of these things are ridiculous. How can I say I don't want to see the Prime Minister of Britain? Jimmy is my friend, he is a personal friend, and I am talking about Rhodesia. I went to the United States to talk about Rhodesia. How can I refuse to talk about Rhodesia to Jimmy here? It is ridiculous. I don't know who is spreading this story! I have made these thousands of miles to talk about Rhodesia, then I come here and I refuse to talk to Jimmy about Rhodesia. Who suggests this?

PRESS: The puzzle is that you are not together and the meeting is not taking place, that is all.

PRESIDENT: You ask them why the meeting is not taking place! Don't ask me. I am here. I was there, I have just had talks with Secretary Vance on Rhodesia. And who is suggesting that I am refusing to see the British on Rhodesia?

PRESS: I think the puzzle, Mr. President, is why you were not going, say, the twenty five miles to Chequers from the airport.

PRESIDENT: It is twenty five miles either way.

PRESS: Mr. President, when do you expect to see the Anglo-American package presented? Have you a feeling that it would be this month or next month?

PRESIDENT: I do not know.

PRESS: The Americans appear to be anxious to do it soon!

PRESIDENT: I think they are. I think the Americans are moving in with a sense of urgency. I am very pleased and I see that they are very serious. I am very pleased about their seriousness.

PRESS: Mr. President, it would seem in this serious situation that you might have some useful role to play in these talks [Chequers]. I am only speaking as an observer and I would like to . . .

PRESIDENT: Which talks? I had talks with President Carter. Frankly I don't understand this thing. I went to Washington to have talks with President Carter on southern Africa. I have done that. The Americans and the British on the other hand have their own talks. They are having these talks. President Carter says to me, 'Look, there will be talks in London with Secretary Vance and the British. Is it possible for Secretary Vance to see you?' I said, 'Yes, I will be passing through London.' So Secretary Vance had seen me to explain to me what they have been talking about. I was passing through here and President Carter asked his Secretary of State to brief me on their discussions here.

I am not scheduled to have any discussions on Rhodesia in London at all. And who is suggesting this? I don't know why he is suggesting it and why my not going to Chequers should be seen as a snub to Mr. Callaghan. I am passing through. I have made a number of appointments to meet people here. So passing through, and having already made a large number of appointments here, it is really a very simple thing to say to a friend, 'Look, brother, thank you very much, but I am passing through and I have other people I am speaking to!'

PRESS: So is it a time-table problem, Mr. President?

PRESIDENT: It is a time-table problem, but it has been changed from being a time-table to snubbing. Me? Snubbing the Prime Minister of Britain? I have been snubbed and I understand snubbing. I don't snub people !!

Later that afternoon, a sulking British Foreign Secretary, David Owen, comes to see Nyerere, and after two hours of talks he leaves Nyerere utterly unhappy, apprehensive and confused about the British position over the removal of Ian Smith and his army and their replacement by a peoples' government and an army based on the liberation forces.

In the midst of the confusion caused at this meeting, Nyerere and his party board a plane for their flight home. Throughout that evening and deep into the night, Nyerere keeps wondering what the British are up to. All these years they have been pleading weakness. Here is American power which, if borrowed, they can use to effect a transition from a colonial situation to Zimbabwe's nationhood. Yet here they are dithering!

THIRTEEN

It is Monday, 15 August. Nyerere has been thinking about this apparent vascillation of the British without discovering why. But he has decided on a course of action. He calls in the British High Commissioner and the American Ambassador to Tanzania together and tells them about his concern over the British position, or lack of it. He asks for a clarification. The American position on the removal of Ian Smith and his army and their replacement by an elected government and an army based on the liberation forces is confirmed. The British position remains most unclear.

Later that day Nyerere calls a news conference to tell Tanzania, Africa and the world about the outcome of his mission to the U.S.

PRESIDENT: I have been on a state visit to the United States. It was both a state visit and a business visit. My business was on southern Africa. I went there because as a result of the statements which both President Carter himself and some of his colleagues have been making on the problem of southern Africa, I felt perhaps it is possible to get the United States to assist us now in resolving these problems of southern Africa.

Before explaining to you my summary of the discussions which I had with President Carter and some of his colleagues, I want to summarize in particular the problem of Rhodesia as I see it; and its solution.

At one time all we were demanding from Britain was a declaration that legal independence in Rhodesia would not be granted except on the basis of majority rule. We called that demand NIBMAR (No Independence Before Majority Rule). Happily that time is gone. The British now agree that, in fact, legal independence in Rhodesia should be on the basis of majority rule.

There was a time when if any negotiated settlement had been reached between the British and Smith on the one hand, if you like, and the Nationalists on the other, it would have been possible to reach majority rule on the basis of a qualified franchise, provided that the qualifications were liberal enough to have a sufficiently large number of African voters on the voters' roll to enable them to decide the elections and, therefore, get majority rule.

That time is gone. It is gone through no fault of the Nationalists, because at one time the Nationalists were ready to accept a qualified franchise. As late as 1974/75, we ourselves were urging the Nationalists to accept a qualified franchise. I, personally, kept saying to the Nationalists that we in Tanganyika achieved independence without one-man-one-vote. We introduced one-man-one-vote after independence. At independence our constitution was on the basis of a qualified franchise.

That time has gone because Smith was intransigent. I find that the British and the Americans talk now the language which we talk. They talk not only on the basis that independence in Rhodesia should be on majority rule, but that this majority rule should be on the basis of one-man-one-vote.

I found President Carter even more advanced on this matter than myself at least in his own phraseology. I say one-man-one-vote and President Carter says one-person-one-vote.

There was a time when if a negotiated settlement had been reached through an ordinary constitutional process, the new government of Zimbabwe would have inherited the entire power structure, including the army. That is what happened in Northern Rhodesia or in Nyasaland or in Tanganyika.

A new government comes, replacing the colonial government. And the new government in actual fact inherits the entire power structure. One of the functions after independence may be to change that power structure, but in actual fact you inherit that power structure including the armed and the security forces. So if through constitutional process, through negotiations, independence had been achieved in Rhodesia, the new government of Zimbabwe would have inherited the entire power structure, including the army. That time is gone—it is not possible now. It was no fault of the Nationalists. Smith was responsible.

There was a time, I believe frankly as late as 1975/76, it was possible if a negotiated settlement had been reached to incorporate some elements of the Smith army into the new army of independent Zimbabwe, although the new army would have been basically ZIPA. In fact, last year when they were debating in Geneva, one of the points at issue was WHO was going to be responsible for defence and law and order.

It was assumed that the defence forces or security services would remain intact, at least during the transition to independence. And the question that was being debated was who was actually going to be responsible for that. Smith was saying they must appoint white ministers to be responsible for Internal Affairs and for Defence, and the Nationalists were saying 'No'. But actually the debate was not on whether the Smith army was going to be removed or not, but who was going to be the Minister for Defence?

Now I say that time is gone. So what is the issue now then? The issue now is no longer NIBMAR. The issue now is no longer whether independence is going to be on the basis of a qualified franchise or not a qualified franchise. We are now agreed with the British and everybody that independence in Rhodesia is on the basis of majority rule, one-man-one-vote.

The issue now is the removal, no longer of just Smith, as it would have happened in an ordinary election.

When we say Smith must go out, we now mean Smith including his army. The new army of Zimbabwe is the army now which is fighting Smith. That is the army which is fighting to win the independence of that country and later to be the army of independent Zimbabwe.

We defined this present objective at the Commonwealth

Conference, and to make it clear, I will read to you what the Commonwealth Conference did say. This is the communique of the Commonwealth Conference which was held in London in June this year.

'Heads of Governments recognize that a genuine settlement must involve agreement, not only on appropriate constitutional changes but also on practical measures to ensure the transfer of effective power to a majority government. In this connection they express their deep conviction that a negotiated settlement must entail not only the removal of the illegal Smith regime, but also the dismantling of its apparatus of repression in order to pave the way for the creation of police and armed forces which would be responsive to the needs of the people of Zimbabwe and ensure the orderly and effective transfer of power. Heads of Governments, however, recalled that so far all efforts to achieve a negotiated settlement had foundered on the sustained intransigence of the illegal regime.'

So, at present this is the object. When we say Smith must go we mean that army must go. And the question is whether that army will go through a prolonged fighting between the Smith army and ZIPA—until the independence army wins victory as happened in the case of Mozambique and Angola and Guinea Bissau—or whether we can mobilize Western pressures to achieve the same objective. Hence the war ends, Smith goes, the army goes and then we have the processes of elections and so forth and an elected government is brought into being before independence for Zimbabwe.

My purpose in the United States, therefore, was to find out whether we can get the American understanding first of all that this is the objective. And secondly, whether we can get American pressures to enable us to reach this objective.

So now I can summarize and say; I found President Carter very genuine in his desire to see that majority rule is achieved in southern Africa. I found that having explained these objectives to him, I was able to leave convinced that the Americans are willing to throw their weight behind the British, because after all the British are the colonial power there. The Americans are willing to throw their weight behind the British to enable these objectives to be achieved. I say, I left the United States after my discussion with President Carter and his colleagues, in no doubt at all about their genuineness, their determination, their sense of urgency; if others also can show the same sense of urgency.

I passed through London. We had since June agreed in the Commonwealth that these were the objectives. It is quite clear in London they know that these are the objectives. I did not leave London, on the other hand, feeling that there is a similar sense of urgency there, as I found in Washington. Whether I misjudged the situation, I don't know!

In fact, I left London a little confused. The objectives are known; they were argued in the Commonwealth and accepted by all the Commonwealth. But I left London a little confused and now I am engaged in finding out if I can get more clarifications from London on how we go about to achieve these objectives which we now say we accept. And this clarification from London is important because it is not enough that American determination should be sincere, honest and firm. The Americans can only work through the British. I don't assume that they could work on their own. Actually I think at one time they said they cannot work on their own.

So it is important to be quite sure that the British have the same sense of urgency, that we have the same understanding before one can be quite sure that the way ahead is clear. When I left Washington I thought the way ahead was very clear. When I left London I din't feel the way ahead was as clear. I was a little more confused. Since my arrival here I have received a message from President Carter. This confirms again the Washington position. It has not removed my little confusion I have about London. So, I think in the next few days we will be engaged in finding out whether I was right or wrong to leave London with a little confusion.

Gentlemen and ladies, I think I have said enough. Now if you want to ask questions, fine.

PRESS: Mr. President, as far as your talks with President Carter are concerned, if I summarize what you have said and what President Carter was quoted as saying in Washington . . . he said you were almost reaching agreement on the goals and purposes of the diplomatic efforts that were made as far as southern Africa was concerned, particularly Rhodesia. Could you elaborate on this almost complete agreement; were there areas of disagreement?

PRESIDENT: You realize I have confined myself to Rhodesia.

PRESS: Yes.

PRESIDENT: But actually we discussed Rhodesia, we discussed Namibia and at one time we discussed Angola. I think at the end of the discussion on Angola, it was President Carter who said, 'Mr. President, I am very pleased that we have discovered something on which we disagree'.

PRESS: What is the area of disagreement?

PRESIDENT: Well, now, don't you realize I have been talking about Rhodesia? Let us not go to Angola.

PRESS: Now, given the tentative commitment by the Americans and the slight confusion from the British, do the two areas of confusion and genuineness by the Americans indicate any change of our approach to the Rhodesia problem?

PRESIDENT: No. I mean what change? Look, there is fighting and every time I'm asked, 'Do you believe in a peaceful solution, Mr. Nyerere, to the Rhodesian problem?' I say, 'What is a peaceful solution?' There is fighting now, people are fighting. I did try in many years to get a settlement without fighting. It is not possible now to talk about a peaceful solution; what you can talk about now is how quickly we do end that war.

My purpose is really trying to get American power behind the liberation struggle. To get American power so that we can shorten that war. We shall go on as usual to help the Freedom Fighters to intensify the war. I have said this in the United States openly. I shall go on seeking support, from those who can give us support, so that if possible a combination of the escalation of the war, and an escalation of whatever pressure the Western powers can put together, can shorten the period of this war.

I will go on on the one hand, together with my colleagues, helping the freedom fighters to intensify the war. And on the other I will go on, non-stop, to mobilize the other forces wherever I can get them, including pressures from the Western countries and from the United States. And I repeat, I found a refreshing seriousness in the United States administration on the question of southern Africa.

PRESS: Mr. President, the genuineness of the Americans and the confusion of the British have nevertheless produced a new peace plan introducing majority rule in Rhodesia. Is this not also confusing?

PRESIDENT: No. I don't know what is confusing. They are all agreed. I think this agreeing is completely genuine, including the British. When the British now say, they do accept majority rule, they are completely genuine. I don't think they are fooling anybody. Because in any case there is no other way now.

So the British are genuine when they say they will not legalize independence in Rhodesia except on the basis of majority rule. They are agreeing with the Americans that independence should be preceded by elections, and elections should be on the basis of one-man-one-vote. On this one there is no confusion.

It is really how do we get there. I was not even talking about the constitution. We are agreed—the constitution is going to be on one-man-one-vote. This was not what we were discussing. When we say Smith must go, he must go because he is a stumbling block. This is the issue; Smith is a stumbling block. The British had been saying, 'Look, you people. We have no power. If we had power in Rhodesia, as we had in Tanganyika, in Kenya and in Nigeria, we would have decolonized. If we had power we would have removed Smith.'

The British have been arguing or pleading, or whatever you like. They have been pleading weakness all the time. 'It is Smith who has the power. We don't have any power. And we have no power to remove him.' This is what really the British have been saying. And this emphasis on negotiations has been, 'Since we have no power to remove him, we can only negotiate; we can only be nice to him until he relinquishes his power.'

We have always said, being nice to Smith will never bring independence. You can't negotiate independence with Smith. Majority rule can only come by force. You have to force Smith out of power. You can't smile him out of power, this is not possible. So, I am completely convinced that the British now are genuine in their saying they accept majority rule, and majority rule on one-man-one-vote. This is not our issue. Our issue is what do we do in the specific issues? How do we go about removing the stumbling block—Smith and his power structure, in particular the army? It is there where I say you do expect this clarification to come from Britain but you don't get this clarification. When you probe this you end up with confusion.

PRESS: Mr. President, does the genuineness of the Americans get to the point that they are prepared to use force?

PRESIDENT: Now, I can't argue with the Americans; I said the British plead weakness. The whole purpose of this exercise is to put power behind the British, and I think the Americans are quite genuine when they say they are ready to co-operate in putting as much power behind the British as the British will ask for.

PRESS: Mr. President, can you tell us a little more precisely what was precisely the source of your confusion as far as the British are concerned in this?

PRESIDENT: I am not quite sure. Before I left here I was told that there were detailed plans. Now, for me detailed plans with regard to Rhodesia must be detailed plans to remove Smith and his power structure, in particular the army.

We have already all of us agreed about this objective in the Commonwealth. So, if now I am told that the British and the Americans are ready, I believe they are ready to solve this problem. I don't expect the Americans to tell me this. I want to know whether the Americans will help the British to achieve this objective. So, I really want to find out from the British what they mean if they are ready. And I say I don't find a satisfying answer.

PRESS: Ndugu President, I do not want to be indulgent, Sir, about the Americans, but you are quoted by the American press as having expressed the interest of the Africans to have arms from the United States. Now, two things: one, what was the response from the Americans? And, two, whether out of this genuineness of the Americans, you think they are in a position to help the Freedom Fighters with arms?

PRESIDENT: I said, and I repeat it, once we have come to the conclusion that an armed struggle is necessary, and since we don't make arms, I will get the arms from anywhere. So, if while I was in Washington I had been offered arms I would have said thank you very much, and unless, of course, they had told me take the arms but say nothing. I would have published this without any inhibition at all!

But the Americans have inhibitions and I don't embarrass friends. I know that they will not give me arms. So, I don't go to America to seek for arms. Once I have heard that President Carter is now willing to throw American weight behind the liberation movement I must ask for whatever they can give within their limitations. And in spite of their limitations, they are still very powerful. If the Western powers decide that the racist and minority regimes in southern Africa should go, they go. They don't actually have to use arms at all. They need simply to be very serious, and those regimes would go. A combination of lack of support for them from the United States and guerrilla fighting would end those regimes there. So I didn't ask for arms from the United States. Why, should I?

PRESS: Mr. President, so what role will the Americans have in the establishment of the government of Zimbabwe?

PRESIDENT: I will put it this way—that historically the British are the power in Rhodesia. I wouldn't have to worry about decolonization there, nor would the Russians. They give us arms but they will not actually go there and do anything. You could just as well say, what exactly are the Russians going to do in the establishment of a new government? They won't. They won't do anything in establishing a new government there. But they are helping. They are giving us the arms and these arms will assist in removing Smith and his power structure.

So I go to the United States, and say, 'You can't give me arms, but really you are very powerful, you can sanction these people. You can apply all sorts of pressure.' They know what kind of pressures they can apply. We will talk to the British because they are the colonial power. We will give arms to the liberation movement but we will talk to the colonial power and whatever pressures they need to fulfil their obligation, their responsibility as a colonial power, we will give them. I don't believe therefore that the Americans themselves would be playing a role in establishing a government there. My purpose is to collect a combination of pressures, not to invite the Americans to go and help to form a new government, any more than I am asking the Russians to go and form a new government there. Actually sometimes this is what is said—because I take arms from the Russians, they think I am asking the Russians to go and form a government of Zimbabwe. Now I am asking for American pressure. I am not actually asking the Americans to go and form a new government in Zimbabwe, at all. I am collecting pressures against Smith.

PRESS: Mr. President, are you planning to call a summit to review the progress shortly with your colleagues?

PRESIDENT: I certainly want to brief my colleagues, about my discussions with President Carter and his colleagues and also my discussions in London. But, I don't have to call a summit. I can brief my colleagues without calling a meeting.

PRESS: Ndugu President, did you leave Britain confused because during your discussions you realized that you were diverting from the Commonwealth communique?

PRESIDENT: I say, because we had already agreed on the objective, and because really the British are the ones who are going to be responsible in achieving a clearly defined objective, and because before going out I was told that they have proposals which are ready in order to solve this, I expected from the British a clarity, and I did not find this clarity.

PRESS: Ndugu President, taking you a bit from Rhodesia; during your state visit in the United States, you went around and saw the state farms and other activities.

PRESIDENT: State farms in the United States? (*Laughter*). Okay, you ask your question.

PRESS: I don't know what you have learnt from the Americans that can be of help to Tanzania. Secondly, you have not covered your visit to Canada and Jamaica I don't know if you can brief us a bit on these.

PRESIDENT: No, I don't want confusion. You see, really I want some clarity also. My purpose is really to try and get some clarity about these major issues.

I saw farms. You know the Americans are very advanced in all these things. I asked them before I went, that since they were kind enough to allow me a few days after my talks with the President, I would like to go round. But I said beforehand, I was not interested in industry, because if they show me their industry I will be so impressed, I will not be able to learn a thing. But I said farming is farming. It does not matter how advanced it is. . . .

PRESIDENT: Ahsante sana. Thank you very much.

FOURTEEN

Saturday of that week, Nyerere calls another news conference. After a flurry of diplomatic activity, he has

had further visits by the British and American envoys coming together, to assure him that the British position on Ian Smith and his army is now similar to that of the Americans. He tells the media that his 'confusion' arising out of the London meeting with Owen has now been cleared.

PRESIDENT: Gentlemen, I think I need to apologize to you for spoiling your week-end, but I thought after what I had said to you five days ago, it might be useful if I saw you again as soon as possible.

You will remember that when we had a press conference five days ago, I tried to explain to you the purpose of my visit to the United States, in particular with regard to our problem of Zimbabwe and that I was satisfied with my discussions with President Carter on the solution to the problem of Zimbabwe. But after my discussion with the British in London I left with a little confusion. I said I was therefore hoping for some clarification from the British side in order to remove this little confusion of mine.

It might be useful if I try to summarize again what the issue is and as we see it. I think at present if you leave out Smith we are all agreed. When I say all I mean the British, the Americans, the Nationalists and we of the Front Line States. I hope therefore the O.A.U. are agreed that Zimbabwe should become independent on the basis of majority rule on a constitution based on one-man-one-vote. We agreed on that—there is no debate among those I have mentioned. There is really no debate now about that.

I think I did try to say the other day that if a settlement like this had been reached before now—in fact I think I said: if a settlement had been reached which did not even reach that one-man-one-vote, but a qualified vote which was able to bring about majority rule—the new majority government, the new African government, could have inherited the total power structure of present Rhodesia. Then they might have taken time to change it.

But they would have inherited the army, the police, the civil service and the economy. They would take time to change that structure. But the assumption was if a settlement had been reached, a year ago or two years ago, the present power structure would have been inherited. So, at present the issue is no longer the form of the constitution. The issue is the army. At present we are saying that when we say Smith must go, we mean Smith and his army must go. Because the people of Zimbabwe have already decided; they are now training an army. The young men are leaving schools, farms and factories so as to be trained to remove Smith and his army.

The people of Zimbabwe have already made up their minds to train an army whose purpose is to defeat Smith and then become the army of independent Zimbabwe. That decision has been made. The decision that had not been made is about the future of the government of Zimbabwe. I think we are all agreed that there is going to be elections there. I am told the Bishop thinks he will get 90 per cent of the votes; Sithole thinks he will get 90 per cent of the votes; the Patriotic Front think they will get 90 per cent of the votes—that is really their own business.

As far as voting is concerned, the decision is in the future. The decision as to whom of those factions is going to form the government of independent Zimbabwe is in the future. The decision as to the army of independent Zimbabwe has been made. That army is now being trained. That army will either by itself alone without any assistance from the international community get rid of Smith and become the army of independent Zimbabwe; or with the assistance of the international community might end the war much more quickly and get rid of Smith and become the army of independent Zimbabwe. Now that is the issue.

I thought that in Washington I had made this position clear. This position had been made very clear at the Commonwealth Conference in June; and all the Commonwealth countries including Britain had accepted that position. My purpose in going to the United States was to try and find out, since the Americans and the British were co-operating in evolving a solution of the Rhodesian problem, whether the Americans also understood this essential point, that Smith and his army must go. Having explained this in the United States, I found that President Carter and his colleagues understood it and accepted it.

I went to London where the Commonwealth conference had taken place, and then it is in London where I got the confusion. I told you, I was seeking for a little more clarification. Since I had put this doubt to you, I think it is fair that I should now tell you that I have received information both from Washington and London. Both the British High Commissioner and the American

Ambassador saw me to clarify this point. On the basis of this clarification, I believe we are agreed on the essential point. The essential point is Smith's army has to be removed and the future army of independent Zimbabwe has to be based on the present army of the Patriotic Front.

I thought I should make that point clear myself, because I had raised these doubts myself. Perhaps, having said that I shouldn't say any more, because this is the only clarification I really wanted to make to you.

PRESS: The British are the ones who created the confusion about which you have sought the clarification. Now, apart from the clarification, has there been any indication on the part of the British to go further than what they have committed themselves to on the removal of Smith? Are they really prepared now to engage in physically removing Ian Smith?

PRESIDENT: I really don't want to go into those details. I want to be quite sure that we are agreed on the objective. So, as far as I am concerned, those are the details which they can then explain. I am not pressing. It is not my function to press the British or the Americans about the details they have worked out in achieving this objective. My function is to make sure that we have the same objective in mind. I have at least explained this objective to them, and it is understood and accepted.

The only thing I would like to say and it is only a repetition because I have said it before, but I think there is no harm in my saying it, is that I believe President Carter and his colleagues are genuine. There is no harm in my saying this. I believe President Carter and his colleagues are committed to getting majority rule in Rhodesia. I am saying this for two reasons; one could say three but I say two reasons.

One, President Carter is a completely honest person. Secondly, he is a true liberal—an ordinary true liberal. I did not go to Washington to ask for socialism in southern Africa. When my friends talk about socialism I say, 'Look, one of my functions here is to fulfil the objectives of the O.A.U. in southern Africa. The Liberation Committee is here on behalf of the O.A.U. It has a function. That function is not socialism; it is liberation.'

So when we meet whether it is in Libreville or even in Kampala, we are talking about liberation—not socialism. It is not the function of the Liberation Committee or my function or the function of the Patriotic Front to talk about socialism in Africa. We are not talking about socialism, whatever our policies may be within our own countries. So I did not go to Washington to ask for socialism. It is not my function to go to Washington to ask for socialism. I did go to Washington to ask for support to get the end of minority rule in southern Africa and the end of racialism in southern Africa.

I say President Carter is an honest person and he is an ordinary liberal. I don't believe I embarrass President Carter when I ask him for support to end racialism and to get regimes established on the basis of one-man-one-vote. I believe Smith would embarrass President Carter. I believe Vorster would embarrass President Carter; not myself when I ask him not to support continued racialism and minority rule in southern Africa. Not the Five Front Line States when we ask President Carter to support ordinary democratic processes. I believe President Carter and his colleagues are completely genuine. President Carter is an honest person and he is a liberal—that is one.

Secondly, I believe it is possible for the United States, including reactionaries in the United States, to come to the conclusion in 1977, when Mozambique is independent and Angola is independent and the Portuguese have gone, it is possible to come to the conclusion that they should no longer support minority rule and racialism in southern Africa. Because if they do, they will lose. It is not in their interests. They have a situation like an Angola situation or a Mozambique situation and it happens that those reactionaries think that the Angola situation and the Mozambique situation is not very good for them.

I believe for those reasons that President Carter is completely genuine in wanting to see a change in southern Africa on one-man-one-vote where the Africans can begin to run their governments. If you want to go and talk about socialism, you go, I am not going. I am only talking about liberation in those terms. I believe that given that position it is possible now to push forward a little bit. I think it is possible to move a little bit.

PRESS: Mr. President, Sir, can I ask about the diplomatic row between Tanzania and France?*

---

* The French Foreign Minister, M. De Guiringuad, cancelled a visit to Tanzania in mid-August 1977, after Dar es Salaam University students staged a protest at the airport against the supply of arms to South Africa by the French government.

PRESIDENT: I don't know what you want to ask about the diplomatic row between Tanzania and France. We were quite happy to receive the Foreign Minister of France. France does sell arms to South Africa. Of all the Western countries, France is now the biggest supporter of racialism in southern Africa. France has many friends in Africa. It is very difficult to criticize the French at the O.A.U. because they have so many friends there. But France is arrogant. France is defiant. France is mercantile in its relations with Africa.

So, all the students were doing was to say to France, 'Why do you sell arms to South Africa?' That is all they were doing in posters. Then the French in their usual arrogance about Africa asked us to apologize. The French are selling arms to South Africa daily; daily people are dying in South Africa. The French are arming that racialist regime. The Foreign Minister of France comes here and we hope we can sit down and find an opportunity to discuss why the French are doing this. Our students are simply asking in posters. The French cannot tell me that they are not used to posters asking these questions.

Then the French ask the government of Tanzania to apologize. It is not the French who are going to apologize to us for selling deadly weapons to South Africa where there is a racist regime which is killing our people daily! They ask us to apologize. They try to make a distinction and ask us to regret. Okay. If there is a distinction between apology and regret, then the French should be the first ones to regret to us that they are selling arms to South Africa.

But they are going round saying we have been selling arms. Now, after the present contracts are out we will stop without any regret. Then they ask the government of Tanzania to apologize or at least to regret, or otherwise the dignity of France has been hurt by these posters. The dignity of Africa is not being hurt at all by this racism, this arming of South Africa, no! But the dignity of France is being hurt by students asking why France is arming this racist regime. I think really it is going a little too far.

PRESS: Mr. President, I have two questions. One, whilst you are a strong believer of President Carter's intentions, I am not so sure that you feel very much the same with the British government's stand. Now, that you had doubts for quite some time . . .

PRESIDENT: I am now clarifying that I feel satisfied. I expressed those doubts but since then I received a joint message from both the British and the Americans trying to remove my doubts. I am saying frankly that my advice both to the British and to the Nationalists is: we have all faced this problem of Rhodesia now for years. The British have faced this problem; we have faced this problem.

President Carter can say, 'It is not my problem. It is your problem, you people.' He could. But I don't think really the British can afford to say, 'It is not our problem; it is their problem.' I can't afford to say it is not our problem. It is our problem. In fact, I can't wash my hands. I have heard some people in Britain say, 'Nothing would make us happier than to wash our hands.' I don't know who can wash their hands off this problem in Britain.

Having sat in the Commonwealth conference and found that objective so clear, having got American support so clearly committed to that objective, my advice to the British and to the Nationalists is to read Shakespeare's Julius Caesar—'There is a tide in the affairs of men . . .'* All my friends now should seize this tide, get this problem of Rhodesia out of the way without going on dithering and being clever. Really what is the use of trying to be clever now? The Commonwealth countries have sat down and decided on the objectives. We have agreed upon those objectives. How many nations were in London? We have American support behind this objective. We should really now be completely honest and get rid of this problem; and not really going around being a little clever. Why be clever? We should get rid of this problem.

PRESS: Mr. President, are you calling a meeting with your colleagues of Front Line States?

PRESIDENT: I am not calling a meeting but I am hoping, on the basis of this clarification, it will be possible for President Kaunda to call a meeting. President Kaunda may call a meeting.

PRESS: Mr. President, are you convinced that the United States and Britain will no longer try to divide the Nationalist forces in

---

* There is a tide in the affairs of men,
Which, taken at the flood, leads on to fortune;
Omitted, all the voyage of their life
Is bound in shallows and in miseries.
(*Julius Caesar*, Act IV, Scene III, lines 216-19)

Zimbabwe—both the Patriotic Front versus the Muzorewa/ Sithole factions?

PRESIDENT: There are some ideas that a solution of the Rhodesian problem could be based on Muzorewa and Sithole, who are some of the prophets of this solution. They say they have the votes. Smith has the guns so they should come together. Sithole and the Bishop, so it is said, have the votes, Smith has the guns and if those two can form an alliance this alliance would be the solution. This is what is called the internal solution.*

My understanding is that both the Americans and the British have said to those concerned (and those concerned are supposed to mean Smith), that the internal solution would not be acceptable to them. As far as I am concerned, I don't want to follow that. I am saying what I stand for and if the Nationalists want to be divided that is their own business. Because there will be people who will try to divide the Nationalists. What can I do? But these Nationalists should behave like adults. They should refuse to be divided. But I can't stop attempts.

Thank you, gentlemen.

FIFTEEN

Those doubts cleared, the way is then paved for Nyerere to ask his colleagues of the Front Line States to a meeting in Lusaka, on 27 August. This is the meeting at which the British Foreign Secretary, David Owen and the American Ambassador to the United Nations, Andrew Young, brief the Front Line Presidents on the major ingredients of the proposals on Rhodesia, due for publication on 1 September under an Anglo-American banner.

But at the Lusaka summit, Dr. Owen falls back to his Heathrow position. This appears to put Andrew Young in a fix. For this was clearly not what the Americans had been made to expect. Yet Rhodesia is a British problem. Theirs is the duty to decolonize and America's role is to back up

* Smith, Muzorewa, Chirau and Sithole signed the so-called 'internal settlement' on 3 March 1978, but the war has since intensified.

the British by giving them American teeth with which to bite Smith.

At the end of that meeting, Nyerere addresses the news media, and studiously avoids answering questions on the proposals.

PRESIDENT: Ladies and Gentlemen, the meeting we held today was not a usual one. As you know, we had the representatives of the British government and the American government. It is useful to us to say a few things after our meeting. It is not easy for us to satisfy you people after this kind of meeting but to the extent that it is possible, it is useful to clarify some of these matters.

You have to forgive me if I go back to give some historical perspectives. It is assumed that we are reaching a crucial period in southern Africa in general and Rhodesia in particular. We shall sometimes agree and sometimes disagree about some matters we discuss. It is important to have the historical perspective in order to see who is to blame.

I have said before and I repeat that somebody will have to say to Smith and the Whites in Rhodesia in general, and that somebody will have to be a friend of the Whites, that it is impossible in history to recall lost opportunities. When an opportunity has gone, it has gone; you cannot recall it. It is easy to lose other opportunities, even present ones. The Rhodesians have in the past lost lots of opportunities.

In this very room, some three years ago, we urged the Rhodesian Nationalists to agree to a constitution short of one-man-one-vote. President Kaunda and myself were urging the Nationalists to agree to a limited franchise. We failed. Not because the Nationalists were not accepting a limited franchise but Smith would not accept it.

Now we are talking of one-man-one-vote. In Washington President Carter was emphasizing this to me and he was saying one-person-one-vote. We are now all agreed that a settlement in Rhodesia will have to be based on one-man-one-vote. That opportunity for a qualified franchise has gone. It was not lost by us. If it was wanted by the Whites in Rhodesia, they lost it. Their leaders were so stubborn.

Two years ago, possibly even less than two years ago, when

we were so keen to have a negotiated settlement, we talked to the South Africans. In one of the rooms behind here President Kaunda, President Khama and myself talked to South African and Rhodesian officials.

Eventually, President Kaunda had to meet Vorster. We were so keen to reach a negotiated settlement. Had a negotiated settlement been reached, say two years ago, there was hardly any doubt that the new government of independent Zimbabwe would have inherited the entire power structure built up by the minority government. They would have inherited the army, the police, the civil service and the economy. It would have taken them several years to change the compositions of the minority power structure. That time is gone. We were not responsible. Somebody will have to tell the Whites in Rhodesia that Smith was responsible.

We are now saying and it is important the world should know what we are saying, it is still possible for the new government of independent Zimbabwe to inherit that civil service, that police and that economy which is basically dominated by the White minority. That would change over time. It is not likely to change on independence day.

But we are saying it is no longer possible for the new government of Zimbabwe to inherit the army of Smith. It is now a truly enemy army. That army has to go. If that opportunity is going to be lost again we will not be responsible. I am saying people who believe they are friends of Whites in Rhodesia must tell them they still have an opportunity. They can stay in that country. But when we are thinking of the institutions of a future Zimbabwe we cannot have in mind the interests of racists who are going to be leaving that country in any case. We have to be thinking of Whites who are going to be prepared to live in that country under a majority government.

But we talk as if we have to consider the views of a bunch of rebels and racists and if we don't satisfy them then a settlement is not possible. But we are dealing with rebels!

So the present discussion centres on the future army of Zimbabwe. The Zimbabweans have not elected their government; we hope a day will come when they will elect their own government. We are saying the people of Zimbabwe have made up their mind about their army. We can't say they have not decided about their army. That decision they have made. They have taken up arms and they are fighting the rebel army.

They can take five, ten and even twenty years. Eventually they will defeat that army and they will then become the army of independent Zimbabwe. These people are interested in the liberation of their country not in protecting their standards of living. They are willing to take a long time but that is the objective. They will have to defeat that army. If our Western friends are interested in helping us, they can help us to achieve the objective in a shorter period. We cannot agree to a settlement which entrenches, gives respectability to and simply legalizes the Smith army. We can't accept an argument which simply says, 'You will line up the Smith army and ask them to take an oath of allegiance.'

So we are seeking for assistance from the international community. Our function is to seek for assistance from the international community behind the Nationalists whose young men are now dying for the liberation of their own country. We are seeking the international community to help us to achieve that objective—to get rid of this rebel army which if the British had the power and the political will, they should have done themselves.

But the Nationalists have been forced to do it themselves. We are seeking for international support for that purpose. If we don't get it we will continue with the struggle. But I repeat, what the Zimbabweans, our colleagues, are working for is a free Zimbabwe, non-racist, where all Zimbabweans of whatever race can live in peace.

If it has not been achieved by now it is not because of the Africans there.

The Whites took over that country since 1923. I was born in 1922. The British say they lost power there since 1923. They have not been able to create a non-racist country. The Africans still want an opportunity to build a non-racist country. To get that opportunity Smith, the leader of racism there, and his army, must go and the West must help us achieve this objective. That is what we are saying.

PRESS: Mr. President, are you objecting to the Anglo-American proposals?

PRESIDENT: We are saying that we will accept the Anglo-

American proposals if they are aimed at helping us to achieve this objective which we have defined very clearly. We defined this objective at the Commonwealth conference. This objective was accepted by the Commonwealth at its last meeting in London. It's part of the official documents of the Commonwealth. So what we want to know is who is objecting to this objective now?

PRESS: Mr. President, could you tell us what the Anglo-American package contains?

PRESIDENT: No, I cannot. I am only telling you that whatever they are we will support them if they are clearly intended to help us to achieve this objective as we have defined. We have defined the objective very clearly because we do not want to be misunderstood on this one. When we now say Smith must go, we mean Smith and his army must go.

In 1974 when we said Smith must go, we meant Smith must go and be replaced by politicians and the power structure would have remained. In 1977, when we say Smith must go we mean Smith and his army. In 1980, when we say Smith must go we shall be meaning Smith and the entire structure. Time is going to change. What I am saying now no Zimbabwe politician will be able to say in 1980 or in 1981 or 1982. They will then be aiming at the destruction of the entire power structure. I am saying some friends of the Whites will have to tell them this. If I say this they won't believe me.

PRESS: Do the proposals call for the removal of the rebel Smith and his army?

PRESIDENT: I am not discussing the Anglo-American proposals. I am saying our attitude to the Anglo-American proposals when they are made public will depend upon whether or not they are intended to achieve this objective which we are defining frankly everywhere, privately and publicly. We do not have two positions on this question of Smith and his army.

PRESS: Mr. President, you said the Smith army must go. Have you any position regarding an international force?

PRESIDENT: I have no position on mechanics. Mechanics can be discussed. I have one position; our function, the O.A.U.'s function, is to get Smith and his army out of the way to enable an elected government to take over in Zimbabwe.

PRESS: Would you accept a combined force to include elements of the disbanded Rhodesian army along with the Nationalists?

PRESIDENT: Would you? I am not a Zimbabwean!

PRESS: Mr. President, do you feel encouraged or discouraged after today's meeting with the British and American representatives?

PRESIDENT: I am saying our attitude is the same. Whatever proposals are made it is going to depend on whether those proposals are going to help us to achieve this objective we have defined.

We defined this objective clearly at the Commonwealth conference in London. It's part of the communique. We have explained this very clearly to our friends in Washington. We do not want to hide this objective. When we were urging our friends to accept a limited franchise, we were not hiding it. We are interested in achieving majority rule in Zimbabwe. We are now, again, defining this objective very clearly. We do not like to be misunderstood. Smith and his army has to go. Whoever wants to help us must help to achieve this objective. If you are not helping us to achieve this objective, you are not helping us. So our attitude to whatever proposals you have will depend on whether you are giving us assistance to achieve this objective.

PRESS: Do you think the proposals you heard today will help to achieve your objective?

PRESIDENT: Now look, have I not told you enough? Do not ask me about the Anglo-American proposals. I am telling you what we on behalf of the O.A.U. are helping the Nationalists in Rhodesia to achieve.

PRESS: What is your reaction to the proposals today?

PRESIDENT: Not today; when they come! When they come our reaction will depend upon what I have explained to you.

PRESS: What happened today then?

PRESIDENT: Today we discussed. (*Laughter*.) We made these points very clear.

PRESS: Mr. President, what will be the future of the Black members of the disbanded Smith army in Rhodesia?

PRESIDENT: What will be their future?

PRESS: Yes.

PRESIDENT: Don't ask me about their future because, in spite of what some people are suggesting, I am not going to form the government of Zimbabwe. I do not know what the government of Zimbabwe is going to say to all those people who were fooled, who were bribed, who were intimidated into supporting rebel Smith. I do not know what the new government is going to do. The new government can give amnesty to everybody. I don't know because there are people now who are serving the Smith regime, Black and White, completely willingly. Others under duress. I don't know. Really, those problems you have to leave to the future government of Zimbabwe.

PRESS: So there will be no guarantee for their safety?

PRESIDENT: What is this safety! Look, at present I am interested in the guarantee of the lives of the people who are dying every day. Not the safety of the people who are killing them!

PRESS: Mr. President, if when they are published the Anglo-American proposals include taking some of the Nationalist forces and some of those forces now under Smith, do you think that would satisfy your requirement that Smith and his army be eliminated?

PRESIDENT: Smith and his army must go. The new government of Zimbabwe will build its own army. Actually they are in the process of building that army now. They are not a government but that army is in the process of being built.

PRESS: Does that mean carrying the Patriotic Front army into power?

PRESIDENT: It is an army. I am talking of an army not power. The government of Zimbabwe is going to be elected by the people of Zimbabwe. But one decision the people of Zimbabwe have already made. They have allowed their sons to take up guns to remove Smith and his rebel army. The decision as to who is going to form the government of Zimbabwe, they have not yet made because they did not get a chance. They will get that chance later.

PRESS: So you are insisting that the Patriotic Front army become the new Zimbabwe army?

PRESIDENT: I am not insisting. The people of Zimbabwe have decided to fight Smith. I am not insisting. I am in Tanzania, my country is independent! The people of Zimbabwe have taken up arms to remove Smith and his army. That decision has been made. Is the international community interested in helping those people to achieve that objective or in sabotaging that objective?

The people of Zimbabwe have not yet had a chance to decide who is going to be President or whether there are going to be twenty presidents or what. But one decision they have made. They are dying already.

PRESS: But if you dissolve the Smith army what army would be put in its place? The Patriotic Front army or some other one?

PRESIDENT: How many do you have? The Patritoc Front has an army. Tell me what other army do you have there?

PRESS: There might be the United Nations Peace-Keeping Force.

PRESIDENT: Is that going to be the army of independent Zimbabwe? I am talking of the army of independent Zimbabwe!

PRESS: Could the army of independent Zimbabwe include people who are now in the current Rhodesian army?

PRESIDENT: I don't know whom it is going to include. I know whom it has now. I know who are forming that army now. Those people work with the Patriotic Front. The people who are determined to remove rebel Smith and his army. I don't know who the new government of Zimbabwe will recruit in that army. It is not my business.

PRESS: Mr. President, from the past experience you have had on the Rhodesian crisis, do you think with the present discussions there is any hope of finding a solution?

PRESIDENT: We are very keen, brother, to find a solution. That is why we travel to London, to New York, to Livingstone, to Moscow and Peking.

SIXTEEN

At nine o'clock Central African time that night (one hour behind East African time), Nyerere and his party board their plane for the two hour flight back to Dar es Salaam. They are due back in Dar es Salaam by midnight. Nyerere instructs his High Commissioner in Lusaka to relay a message to the American Ambassador in Dar es Salaam to be available at Nyerere's home when he lands later that night.

The plane journey back to Dar es Salaam is a repetition of that from London a fortnight earlier, only it is shorter. The question is back again. What are the British up to?

On landing a little after midnight, Nyerere drives straight to his home. There he finds the American Ambassador,

James Spain, waiting. He takes him into his office and tells him what has happened in Lusaka and asks him to relay his concern to Washington.

Later that morning the British High Commissioner, Mervyn Brown, is called in. Nyerere expresses his concern over the British position and seeks a Whitehall clarification.

Following another flurry of diplomatic activity, Nyerere is informed that Owen and Young want to fly to Dar es Salaam to see him once more before 1 September. They come over. In the ensuing audience they confirm that the British do now accept that Smith must go and that this means him and his army. They further confirm that the new army of Zimbabwe shall be based on the liberation forces. Owen assures Nyerere that although this position would not be reflected in the White Paper he was bringing before the British House of Commons, as it was already in print, he would make a statement on the same day, which would cover the clarification that Nyerere has sought and obtained. When that statement is made on 1 September it carries the following paragraph:

With a view to creating one-unified army loyal to the people and government of Zimbabwe, it is stated in the White Paper, at paragraph 11 sub-paragraph (E), that legal provision will be made for the formation of a new body to be called the Zimbabwe National Army. Enrolment in this army will be open to all citizens, but it will be based on the Liberation Forces: it will also include acceptable elements of the Rhodesian Defence Forces. The organization, recruitment and training of this army will be the responsibility of the Resident Commissioner in consultation with the parties concerned. It is self-evident that this army must be loyal to whoever is elected President and whoever forms the government of Zimbabwe, a government chosen on the basis of universal suffrage by an electorate of some 3 million voters, in contrast to the existing situation. Following the elections and prior to Independence, the President-elect will make the decisions on the final structure and composition of the Zimbabwe National Army.

And the White Paper further states that an interim government shall be set up under a British Resident Commissioner; elections on the basis of one man one vote shall be held under the supervision of the Resident Commissioner backed by United Nations forces; that Rhodesia shall become independent in 1978 and that a 1.5 billion dollar fund for the development of Zimbabwe shall be created.

On 25 September, Nyerere calls another summit meeting at which the Front Line States formally react to the Anglo-American proposals. A statement issued at the end of that summit states: 'the Anglo-American proposals have many negative points, leave a number of questions unaswered, but they nevertheless form a basis for negotiations'.

SEVENTEEN

Will the colony of Southern Rhodesia achieve its independence this year? There is no telling.

For there are a number of ifs to which positive answers have to be found, before 1978 can be Rhodesia's year of independence as envisaged in the Anglo-American proposals.

The central issue in Rhodesia has been and remains Ian Smith and his army. All efforts aimed at resolving the problem have had as their object, Smith's removal from power. All the fighting that has been raging has had the removal of Smith and the installation of a peoples' power as its objective. All the fighting that may yet take place has that removal as its objective. All genuine talking that has taken place, or any combination of genuine talking and fighting that may yet take place zeroes in on that objective.

Everything else provided for in the Anglo-American proposals, whatever its seriousness and however important, falls secondary to this central issue. Unless Smith and his power are effectively tackled, everything else in those proposals boils down to nothing. The whole package becomes meaningless. Plus there has been the so-called 'internal settlement' agreement signed on 3 March 1978, between Smith, Bishop Muzorewa, Chief Chirau and Rev. Sithole. This purports to portray Rhodesia as having achieved majority rule but is in fact a sham arrangement under which the minority Whites retain all the power. It has been condemned by the Front Line States, the Patriotic Front and the O.A.U. The United Nations has also rejected it.

So, whether Rhodesia becomes Zimbabwe in the course of 1978 depends first and foremost on the resolution of this problem. And to the extent that the problem is resolved on the basis of the Anglo-American proposals, the onus of removing Smith and his army lies on the British and their American allies. The Nationalists will continue the guerilla war. In the process they will further weaken Smith and to that extent make the task of the British and the Americans of removing Smith relatively less complicated.

But Zimbabwe shall be born. Of that there is no doubt. It is not a matter of whether. It is one of when and how. Now there are two ways. One is that which combines military and non-military pressures such as are envisaged in the Anglo-American proposals. The other is a Zimbabwe that is born of the armed struggle alone. On this latter one, there can be no laid-down date. It could come sooner than the Anglo-American proposals foresee, or later. The success of the armed struggle will be the determinant factor.

If Zimbabwe becomes independent in 1978 largely through the Anglo-American proposals, the 1977 crusade for liberation will have been the major catalyst. It will have achieved total success.

If on the other hand this is not so and independence comes only through fighting, the crusade will, at least, have succeeded in defining and clarifying the issues at stake in Rhodesia. It will still register as a major effort in Africa's long crusade for liberation from alien and racist domination.

Published by Oxford University Press, Maktaba Street, P.O. Box 5299, Dar es Salaam, Tanzania and printed by Tanzania Litho Limited, P.O. Box 200, Arusha, Tanzania.